I DIDN'T HAVE
CANCER
FOR NOTHING

By

Lyn Ellis

1987

RICHARD KAY

80 SLEAFORD ROAD, BOSTON, LINCOLNSHIRE PE21 8EU

© Lyn Ellis 1987

ISBN 0 902662 74 0 'Charity Edition'
ISBN 0 902662 75 9 cased edition
ISBN 0 902662 76 7 paperback edition

The main body of the text has been set on a Xerox 645 in G.B. Boldface P.S.   The newspaper extracts are set in G.B. Square^3 P.S. and the Radio Lincolnshire transcript in G.B. Roman P.S. Italics throughout are in G.B. Boldface Italic P.S.   The body of the text has been reproduced at 90% of the original.   The captions for the illustrations, the title page, the copyright line, and all chapter headings have been set on an Apple- Macintosh Plus with an Apple Laserwriter using the Gestetner Black-cat DTP package.   Printed by Richaprint Ltd., of Priory Road, Freiston, Boston, Lincolnshire on a Solna press.

LIFE IN LINCOLNSHIRE

Books in this series are, just as it says, about life in Lincolnshire. They are not necessarily autobiographical although they are expected to be mainly about the life and work of individual people. They may appear in somewhat varying format although visually compatible as a series. Each title is published in both cased and paperback editions.

Already available:

SOLD: Reminiscences of a Lincolnshire Auctioneer by Henry Brown

MOST BRUTE AND BEASTLY SHIRE by Tom Smallhorn

In preparation:

FROM THE FENS TO WESTMINSTER AND BACK: by Hilda Clarke
    - or WHAT PRICE INDEPENDENCE?

ACKNOWLEDGEMENTS

I have been grateful for, and humbled by, the many kindnesses shown to me by too many people to thank personally. I am glad now to have the chance to place on record my appreciation of all concerned.

Many people have donated to, and raised money for, my Detection of Cancer and Treatment Equipment Fund. Others have been involved as Trustees. Many will be mentioned by name in the book but, whether mentioned or not, and to many whose names I do not even know, my gratitude is very real. To all of them I say thank you from the bottom of my heart.

More particularly for help in the preparation of this autobiography, I say thank you to: George Wheatman for his encouragement and hours spent helping me to put my thoughts on paper; Joan Roseveare, for the kind but perceptive way in which she probed into my life to get the right answers to the right questions; and to Pat Ashberry, not only for agreeing to write the Preface, but also for using her journalistic skills in first launching, and then maintaining public interest in, D.O.C.A.T.E.F.

Both the author and the publisher are most grateful, and wish to express their thanks to: *The Lincolnshire Standard, The Boston Target,* and *Radio Lincolnshire,* for permission to reproduce copyright material which first appeared in their columns or was broadcast by them: to Gary Atkinson, Bob Whitaker, and some unknown photographers, for whose photographs we are most grateful.

The author, the publisher, the DOCATEF Committee, and the Appeal Committee and Trustees of the Boston Stump Restoration Fund wish to express their very real gratitude to all those who have donated their services in the preparation of this book. In particular all are grateful to: **Richaprint** of Freiston for donating all their materials, the associated preparation, and the printing of this book: to **Addys** of Boston for the cover photograph of the Freedom Scroll: and to *The Lincolnshire Standard, The Boston Target,* and *The Spalding Free Press* for their help with publicity and distribution. All services provided from within the South Lincolnshire area have been given free for the initial 'Charity Edition', the only payment needed being for the supply of paper and the cost of binding as neither paper manufacture nor book binding are available from within the area.

CONTENTS

Dedicated to my best friend –
My husband Pat

PREFACE

by

Pat Ashberry

I never imagined, the day I received a letter from a brave Boston nurse recovering from cancer and trying to raise money to help others like herself, that I was to be in at the birth of a legend.

Fanciful words you might think. But how else can I possibly describe Lyn Ellis, the woman who has captured the hearts of countless thousands of people in and around the Boston area with her courageous battle against cancer, a battle she has coupled so movingly with a sustained campaign to raise thousands of pounds to help other victims of the terrible disease?

Lyn is known the length and breadth of the county now for her gutsy approach to life, for her determination to beat her illness, for the humour that keeps her going in spite of the pain and the facial disfiguration she has suffered, and for the way she never stops caring about others, no matter how rotten a day she is having.

Her caring has been the one thing which has kept the cash coming in for DOCATEF (Detection of Cancer and Treatment Equipment Fund), the appeal she started in 1979 after her first major operation, and to date people have given a magnificent £205,000 for equipment at Pilgrim Hospital. That figure is rising weekly.

It was way back in October 1979 that Lyn wrote to me at the Standard asking for a bit of publicity for a fund she wanted to set up.

I'll never forget her words on the phone when I rang her to arrange to go out to Eastville to see her.

"I hope you're ready for this – I look like the back end of a bus!" she said.

Lyn was referring, of course, to her scarred face which, batter-

1

ed and bruised by surgery, was never going to look the same again after surgeons had done their lifesaving job.

I'm not squeamish, but I won't say I wasn't nervous. What was she going to look like? Would I flinch away, be embarrassed?

I needn't have worried. Lyn's welcome was full of warmth. Her operation had blemished her good looks, but it hadn't stopped her smiling, and we hit it off from the word go.

That smile was always there ready to light up her face during an interview that was difficult for both of us - Lyn had to describe the most harrowing details of her illness and operation to a complete stranger, and I had to listen and watch her re-live it all. There were moments when we were both near to tears. But tears are close to laughter, and Lyn's humour saved the day for us.

Since then I've watched her progress as she goes bravely from one operation to the next, always bouncing back, always smiling, always full of praise for Pilgrim Hospital and the folks of Boston, Skegness, Sleaford, Spalding and hereabouts who keep the money pouring in.

It's because of them that the Fund is such a success, she insists, refusing to see that she's wrong - that it's only because of *her*, her guts, her generosity of spirit, her dedication to DOCATEF in spite of her pain, that people are so responsive and generous.

Since those early days Lyn must have talked to thousands of local people about her illness and the Fund, and for them she has done something very special which I reckon is more important than the money.

She's taken that fearful word cancer by the scruff of the neck, dragged it out of the shadows and held it up to the light of day.

In her matter-of-fact way, with touches of Yorkshire humour, she's talked about it, cocked-a-snook at it, even dared to joke about it. And as a result the dreaded Big C doesn't seem to hold quite the fear it used to for Boston people. That's something, in my opinion, for which we have real reason to be grateful to Lyn.

She's been all over the place telling people about her Fund and why she began it. She's been to WI's and slimming clubs, pubs and schools. She even got VIP treatment and supper at one men's group meeting (which shall remain nameless), then at the end of the evening, while waiting for the cheque she'd gone for, discovered she'd been at the wrong place all the time, and no-one had liked to ask her what she had been doing there!

I've listened to Lyn's talk several times and have never failed to be moved by it, even more so, I think, because of her own special brand of humour which she manages to inject into it.

She knows people fight shy of cancer, and there's no way she's going to frighten folks with gory operation details. Instead, she stands there, a slightly eccentric figure with a piratical black patch over one eye - and she makes 'em laugh. They love it, they love her, they love what she is doing and why she's doing it, and the money keeps pouring in.

She quips about the parrot she'd like to have sitting on her shoulder, about the brain scan she's had (they *STILL* haven't managed to find her brain, she says), and about the day she caused havoc at a Lincoln hospital early in her illness trying to cheer up her fellow patients by pulling her nightie over her head and 'streaking' down the length of the ward.

The sister who rushed in to investigate the commotion was NOT, apparently, amused. Lyn just giggles with pleasure at the memory - especially funny to her when she recalls she was about nineteen stones at the time!

Lyn laughs a lot. Knowing her well, as I do now, I know how hard that is for her at times. Her response, whenever I've commented on her remarkable ability to keep on smiling, is typical of her.

"Nobody wants to hear you moaning about how ill you feel," she says. "Besides, fun and laughter are cancer's worst enemies, so it's my way of fighting it."

Another friend of Lyn's said to me the other day: "She's an inspiration to us all."

She certainly is. And I'm sure that while there is a hospital in Boston, and people in it who need help, her spirit will continue to be an inspiration for many generations to come.

Thank you Lyn.

INTRODUCTION

by

George Wheatman

Hilda Clough was born to be ordinary. Any extraordinariness was brought into her life by Lyn Ellis – and that was thrust upon her by that insatiable tumour called cancer, the most dreaded disease known to mankind today, a disease still defying the best medical brains fighting to erase it.

It flourishes where it will, holds no favours for rich nor poor, and once it has established its grasp rarely lets go.

Hilda Clough was born poor and in material things Lyn Ellis has never been well off. But together they have also contrived to cheat the treacherous disease. They have gained strength and friends from the weakness its suffering has caused.

It has, they say, enriched their lives, helped them to inspire other people, and given Lyn an opportunity to bask in the limelight in a way Hilda, in her wildest dreams, never would have thought possible.

Hilda Clough and Lyn Ellis are the same person. Just years and ill health have changed one into the other. The story of both of them is related by Lyn, in her own words, as she tells of her fight against cancer and, with justifiable pride, of the establishment of a fund that has helped many other cancer sufferers.

Lyn touched the hearts of Lincolnshire people when she set up the Detection of Cancer and Treatment Equipment Fund with the aim of providing Boston's Pilgrim Hospital with equipment the National Health Service could not afford, but which many people were desperately needing to use.

These same people have admired the guts and tenacity with which she has steered that fund from one target to another.

4

She has been honoured by her civic leaders, *fêted* by the people, and half blinded and crippled by cancer.

Hilda would not have believed it all possible. Born in humble surroundings, and destined to stay there, she was under confident, in awe of people, and even afraid of the sight of blood.

Lyn, loved by family and friends, thrives on people, has overcome the jolt of countless operations, and become a public speaker of renown through a mouth that is hardly any more her own.

While the name change came with marriage, the personality change came with cancer. From ordinariness to extraordinariness. Lyn would not make the claim herself except to admit that it has been extraordinary the way in which an 'ordinary' person has declared war on this mightiest of enemies and has inspired the public to join her in that fight.

This is the story of a battle - against cancer - but it is also the story of love.

Hilda Clough fell in love at the age of seventeen. When she married Pat he changed both her names. Both changes were something she longed for.

In the early days of their courtship thay shared a tender secret. Too shy to call her darling in public, Pat shortened the endearment to Lyn. "You'll know what I mean," he said.

When they were married, Pat introduced her to everyone as 'Lyn', and Lyn she has remained, a darling to everyone who knows her.

This is her story of suffering and of achievement, and the story of the man who has suffered alongside her - the man who has helped make the pain bearable, the achievements possible. Her husband Pat. He says little and stays in the background, but Lyn's story is his story.

Once, in the early days of the fight against cancer, Lyn was told by a doctor: "We can probably give you another five years." She was excited at the news. All she had to do, she felt, was believe, and she would get better. At the time of telling this story, thirteen years since that first prognosis was given in 1974, she has added another eight years to that estimate of five, celebrated her fiftieth birthday, has seen six more grandchildren come into the world, seen three of her children married, and made many, many friends. "I'm not afraid of dying," she says, "but dread the thought of leaving all my loved ones."

Only once has the constant pain made her feel like giving up the fight. That stage was reached when she felt that she could not face more surgery, and she told her close family that she would let the cancer take its course, let it do what it would with her. She would fight it no more.

She did not make a big thing of that decision and, sadly, the family accepted her wish.

Not so a forthright friend. "You are going to fight it, aren't you Lyn?", she demanded. "So many people rely on you and look to you because you are a fighter."

Lyn replied simply: "Of course I am going to fight it." And the battle continued.

"I'm glad I didn't give up," she said afterwards. "I feel differently now. I don't think I am a special example, but I wouldn't want anything to spoil DOCATEF."

Special? Judge for yourself of a lady whose efforts have inspired the raising of thousands of pounds to enable DOCATEF to purchase this equipment which, should we ever be so unlucky, will give the rest of us a better chance to combat cancer:

Fibre-optic Laryngoscope - this is used to detect cancer in the throat and can be used, without the need to give a general anaesthetic, in the outpatients' department, and so saves the trauma of going to the theatre. It relieves the National Health Service of all the in-patient services hitherto necessary i.e. food, medication, care and cleaning, and frees beds for other surgery patients. It also means that patients are not weakened by anaesthetics and can return to a normal life more rapidly.

Gastroscope - used to detect cancers, ulcers, and other diseases in the stomach. Patients are usually admitted to hospital on one day, given a local anaesthetic, and allowed home the same day.

Sigmoidoscope - used for examining the lower bowel, for cancer detection and other diseases.

Bronchoscope - Patients usually have to go to theatre for examination of their lungs. This is still so, but one specialist said that, with this newest equipment, he had seen parts of the lung he had never seen before

All these 'scopes can be used to take a biopsy, or sample of tissue, and work with the special camera and television screen purchased by DOCATEF, which is invaluable in the training of medical staff.

Bone Marrow Freezer Unit - used to store patient's bone marrow while in remission from some cancers and leukaemia. Patients can be given large doses of drugs which kill the disease but would also destroy the bone marrow. By using this process they can be given back their own bone marrow without rejection. Boston became the first hospital, apart from the big teaching hospitals, to do bone marrow transplants successfully.

Carbon Dioxide Laser - used to treat oral cancer, and cancer in some other parts of the body. It burns the cancer away by means of a laser beam of light. It destroys nerve endings so there is less pain, and seals blood vessels so there is less chance of blood loss. Patients recover much more quickly than when subjected to traditional surgery. It is used mainly by ear, nose, and throat, and by gynaecological surgeons.

Special? Lyn has had too many hospital visits, too many examinations and operations to mention, but judge for yourself the courage needed to overcome these major operations:

P.H. = Pilgrim Hospital

P.H. - 19. 3. 74   to   23. 9. 74
P.H. - 9. 9. 74   to   18. 9. 74   (Fenestration)
P.H. - 5. 4. 76   (Day case)
P.H. - 20. 6. 78   to   21. 6. 78

```
P.H. -  3. 7. 79                      (Day case)
P.H. - 22. 7. 79      to  17. 8. 79   (Maxillectomy)
P.H. - 24. 1. 81
P.H. - 21. 7. 81
P.H. - 14. 8. 82      to  17. 8. 82
P.H. - 29.11. 83      to  30.11. 83
P.H. - 15.12. 83      to  17.12. 83
P.H. -  8. 2. 84      to  20. 2. 84   (Enucleation of eye)
P.H. -  1. 3. 84      to   2. 3. 84
P.H. - 13. 9. 84      to  14. 9. 84
P.H. - 22. 1. 85      to  24. 1. 85
P.H. -  4. 2. 85                      (Removal of remaining
                                       tissues of orbit)

P.H. -  3. 6. 85      to   4. 6. 85
P.H. - 27. 6. 85      to  28. 6. 85
P.H. - 18. 8. 85      to  19. 8. 85
```

King's College Hospital, London:

```
        29.10.80                  (Ethmoidectomy and partial
                                   sphenoidectomy)
        18. 9.83      to  28. 9.83  (Lobectomy)
```

Southampton Hospital:

```
        25. 6.84
        26.11.84                  (in-patient approx. one week)
        22. 4.85                  (Gold vapour laser treatment
```

These are just the 'highlights' - there have been many calls on the skills offered in various hospitals.

Between 1974 and Autumn 1986 Lyn was admitted for investigation, or operation, at Pilgrim Hospital no less than twenty-four times, some were short stays, some were long. In addition to these there was a lengthy spell at Lincoln Hospital; two major operations at King's College Hospital, London; and, on three occasions, admission to hospital in Southampton. Then there were, early in 1986, a couple of days for tests at City Hospital, Nottingham, and in the summer of '86 she was back in Pilgrim Hospital.

8

The pattern has continued into 1987.

Words like fenestration, maxillectomy, enucleation, ethmoidectomy, sphenoidectomy and lobectomy may mean little to most of us. To Lyn they have meant pain and despair . . . and hope. Each has been a major operation, a stepping stone in the rearguard action against cancer.

Special? Who else would have inspired others to walk hundreds of miles, swim countless lengths of pools, give the whole of the salary for over one year from a job, and donate thousands of pounds to so many and so varied fund raising activities.

Lyn Ellis has done all of these things.

And now she has become the first woman to receive the Freedom of the Borough of Boston.

This is her story . . .

1.

THE EARLY DAYS

I SUPPOSE that I have had more time than most to think and reflect on my life, on what has been and what might have been. During my many stays in hospital, or recovery periods at home, I have found that looking back, reminiscing, has been a special kind of therapy, searching perhaps for something that has prepared me for what has become a constant fight against cancer. Maybe, even, looking for something that triggered it off.

I was born under the sign of Capricorn - on the wild, wintry night of January 6th 1937 - and perhaps that was my first bit of luck.

Astrologists say of Capricorns: "They have a superb sense of humour. They take the mickey out of everything, including themselves."

That's true. I have giggled my way through life, and laughed my way through many a pain barrier. An ability to see the funny side of life has perhaps been my biggest asset, but it has also got me into trouble at times.

I can remember an old headmistress telling me: "You are the most happy-go-lucky girl I have ever known." I was just puffing my chest out with pride at such a compliment when she deflated my ego completely by adding: "You have got to snap out of it." I think that was just after I had gained two marks out of a hundred in an algebra test!

I never tired of my mum's stories of the night I was born. To go into the labour ward at the hospital in Bradford she, and an accompanying nurse, had to step outside to cross a small cobbled yard. It was raining and the wind was blowing and the nurse gathered her cloak around her to keep warm, and urged my mother to hurry. Mother laughed and told her: "If its hair gets wet, it will have rust coloured hair like me." So she dallied. She desperately wanted a girl with auburn hair to match her own.

I wasn't born out in the rain, but there were only minutes to spare when mother reached the labour ward. When I popped into this world I had a smattering of blonde hair, and I was cherished from the start.

The time and place of my arrival hardly combined to make a recipe that promised fame and fortune. It was tough for a working-class family in Bradford at a time when there were already rumblings of war, and whilst the future of mankind was soon to be fashioned by far-off battles, a war at home was beginning to shape my future. It was the battles between my mum and dad that turned into this war as their marriage began to crumble.

Father was over-keen on the drink, and often violent towards mother after his drinking evenings. Their fights never involved me, but I was aware that they were happening. After drinking, dad would throw things at mother, at the wall, at anything. I was usually in bed at the time.

I went to Tong Street Primary School in Bradford just before I was five and it was there that I saw my first coloured lady. She was a teacher called Miss Jacob, and I loved her. It would be difficult to live your first five years in Bradford now without seeing a coloured person.

Most Monday afternoons, with the connivance of my mother, I was 'sick' and missed school so that I could go with her to the theatre where the old time variety shows were being staged. Mother loved them, and so did I, as our only luxury of the week. We saw many of the top stars until the headmistress became suspicious about these Monday afternoon illnesses, and mother thought it wiser that I went to school.

I was loved by everyone, and was a happy child. My Aunty Nellie and Uncle Stan, and Aunty Hilda and Uncle Bill, lived down the same street. Cousins Jean, Peter, and Susan were my friends and companions. Oh happy days . . . then mother took me away from all this. Soon I was to carry the name of Davies.

I was about five when a coal wagon drew up at our house and drove us off into the night, my mother, brother Alan, and me. My mother pointed to the driver and said: "This is your new dad." It was Harold. I had met him once before when he came over to talk to me while I was building sand castles in a local park. His daughter was with him and they were just casual to me, but I remembered him when I was lifted into the wagon that night.

The wagon smelt of oil and heat and we all sat in the front. I was on a warm metal cover which vibrated and made me laugh. Already I was laughing on the wrong cue because there was nothing funny about our predicament that night as we hurried to leave, while my real father was working at a munitions factory. We didn't want the neighbours to have the chance of telling him what was happening.

It was a brave decision by my mother to leave father because, in those days, once married you were expected to stay married, and happiness had little to do with it.

For the next few months we lived with first one aunt and then another before eventually moving into a large, dirty, terraced house in Sloane Street, Ripleyville, West Bowling, Bradford.

Meanwhile, my father set up home with Harold's wife - in our old house. An elderly neighbour told me that this swapping of partners made the headlines in the newspapers, but mum and Harold quickly denied it and the neighbour never visited the house again.

Harold was now the man of the house, and I resented him. I remembered my real father well and, as I grew older, I used to look for him in every man of his age. I was never encouraged to talk about him. If I did, it made my mother cry.

My brother Alan had a row with step-father Harold and ran away to live with our father. A court action resulted and I caught sight of my father, briefly, down a corridor, when I accompanied mother to the court. Mother hurried me past and I was too afraid to smile.

I never saw him in person again but, later, I remember seeing him on Alan's wedding photographs. We weren't invited to the wedding but, on the photos, father was just as I had remembered him, tall, over six feet, slim, and his fair hair was brushed back.

When I married and had children myself, I often wondered if father knew about his grandchildren, and used to dream about going to surprise him. But I never did.

Then one day, while we were living at Brocklesby Park, near

Grimsby, mother came to visit. She was in tears and told me that my father had died. She didn't love him any more, and had not done so for a long time, but she was still sad to hear of his death.

Months later we heard that Harold's wife had died. I remember my mother's happiness, not at the news of the death, but because she and Harold were free to marry. She was so excited when she said: "Will you dance at my wedding?"

But it was never to be. Mum died of a heart attack at the age of fifty-two, only a matter of months after the death of Harold's wife.

Harold was a small man who wore glasses and could have doubled for comedian Arthur Askey, except that he seemed a humourless man to me. He ruled the household like a sergeant major, and was never reluctant to aim the odd clout my way if I stepped out of line.

On the day my mother died, Harold showed he had the kind heart I thought was missing when I was young. He delayed telephoning the news because he knew I was alone in the house. He waited until he could contact Pat, and let him break the news to me.

I am sure my step-father tried to be a friend. By nature he was stern, probably because of his own almost Victorian upbringing. "Children should be seen and not heard," was one of his favourite sayings.

Perhaps I should have been more tolerant. The Lyn Ellis of today would have been. The Hilda Clough of that era was more headstrong.

Looking back, there was no doubt that Harold adored my mother, but, until she died, I merely regarded him as her companion and not her husband, nor my father.

After Pat and I were married and lived in Lincolnshire, he would bring mum to see me, either for a day trip on a Sunday or for the weekend: and they always came for Easter. Before she set out mum would telephone to see how many children we were fostering at the time, and would ask their names, so that she could bring each one of them an Easter egg. After mother died we invited Harold for Easter so that he would not be on his own, and, when he arrived, he had an armful of Easter eggs. His eyes were full of tears as he said: "Lilian would have wanted me to do it."

I put my arms round him and gave him a big hug, and I saw Harold in a different light after that. He has kept in touch with the occasional letter and telephone call but now, at the age of seventy eight, lives alone in Yorkshire.

Life was so different from today when I was a child, through the war and then, afterwards, as the country recovered from those distressing years. There was, however, a tremendous neighbourliness in Bradford. We lived in a big council house. There was an air-raid shelter nearby and we often went to sleep in our beds, but woke up in the shelter after having been carried there when the air-raid sirens sounded.

In the shelters everyone sang hymns, drank cocoa, said their prayers, and exchanged stories.

Mother taught me this prayer and insisted that the family kneel together in the shelter to say it:

God is our refuge, be not afraid,
Jesus will keep us all through the raid,
When bombs are falling and danger is near,
Jesus will keep us until the all-clear.

This was the era of the black-out, and much of our life seemed to be lived in darkness. Despite the hardships it was, perhaps strangely, a happy childhood. Now when I look back, the good times seem to outweigh the bad, despite my early brushes with Harold. Our differences were usually over the household chores not being done, or not being done to his satisfaction. Alan used to yell and his punishment was shortlived. I was stubborn, refused to cry, and it was prolonged.

I also had an early introduction to doctors and hospitals. I had scarlet fever at the age of five and was in an isolation ward; at fifteen I broke my coccyx - a bone at the bottom of my spine - and then I broke my wrist and it needed a series of operations to put it right.

Now, as I have been undergoing treatment for cancer by the most advanced methods from the hands of the kindest and most brilliant men, I often reflect ruefully on the day I injured my back.

On leaving Bradford's Usher Street School, I started work in the Co-op laundry offices and, after three weeks at the job, I fell down the office steps. I laughed, picked myself up and ran

14

part of the way home, but later I could not sit down because of the pain. Next day mother sent me to the casualty department of St Luke's Hospital. Despite the pain, I had to walk there on my own. A nurse asked where was my mother, but sister Beryl had T.B. at the time and mum could not leave her. They didn't keep me in hospital, but put me in plaster.

Being encased in that plaster is something I remember as if it were yesterday. There was a pulley from the ceiling and I had to stand with my hands reaching up to this pulley as a nurse and a man in a white coat wrapped the plaster around me, pushing me from one to the other. Then they sent me home and I had to sit in front of the fire to dry out!

Someone at the hospital gave me money to travel home by bus. It was in 1952 and the day King George VI died. Everyone seemed in a state of shock and told each other "The King is dead." I was in a state of shock for a different reason . . . The 'bus conductor was cross because I would not sit down although there were vacant seats.

I was in plaster cast for three months and mother was increasingly anxious for me to go back to work because she needed the money. When I did go back, however, I found I had lost my job in the office. I was offered a place in the laundry, but refused and walked home.

I'm forgetting. There were, in fact, other visits to hospital, even before this. I broke my wrist when I fell out of a tree when playing with a girl from a gypsy family up the street. My reward was a good hiding, because I had been banned from playing with her - the family was thought 'not desirable' - and the break had to be set several times before it was better.

More disobedience resulted in my breaking my wrist again. This time I went over the handlebars of my cycle on the way to school, when I had been told that I should not take the bike to school. I had sneaked it out of the back door.

Then I fell while vaulting in the school gymnasium and dislocated my elbow. I visited hospital for several weeks for physiotherapy treatment. I was really a veteran visitor of hospitals even before I left school, and before I hurt my back.

Breaking my back, however, had a silver lining. As the injury healed I was encouraged to swim and I loved swimming. I went to the pool every morning and every night and became pretty good at it. So good, in fact, that I had high hopes of swimming the channel. I was all set to do just that when I was nineteen - but I got pregnant and married instead.

I had my moments of fun as a swimmer, however, and I swam across Morecambe Bay which, because of the currents one encounters, is a distance of about twenty-one miles.

Memories have come flooding back in the recent years when I have had so much time for thinking and reflecting. Those memories, as with most people I suppose, have brought tears and laughter. The lifestyle was so different from today. Every Monday, wet or fine, was wash day. Every day was nappy-washing day. I used to turn the big wooden mangle while mother folded the clothes, pushed them through the rollers, and caught them on the other side. Before and after school I always had chores to do.

There were big families in every house down the street, on one side Protestants and the other Catholics; mixed marriages were frowned upon.

Guy Fawkes night was a particularly big occasion. Families pooled their resources and gathered round the bonfire to eat roast potatoes, mushy peas, and treacle toffee. We sang our hearts out and no-one left until the last embers of the fire had died. Our eyes were stinging from the smoke and faces were dirty and streaked with tears. You could see similar bonfires and fireworks lighting up the sky from nearby streets.

Mother's baking was superb; she had a reputation for it in the area. If a neighbour was ill, it was mother who was always asked to do the cleaning and baking for the family. When someone died the whole street went into mourning. A door to door collection was taken to help pay for the funeral.

When mum went into hospital to have the three other children, I was moved around a bit. I remember I went to Aunt Hetty's when Gordon was born, but I wasn't happy there. I was forced to play outside when visitors called, while my twin cousins, Patricia and Michael, were bathed and put into their best clothes. Their older sister, Sheila, was kind and felt sorry for me, but I pretended it didn't matter. All I thought of was my new baby brother.

It was different - oh so different - when my sister Beryl was born and I went to my favourite stopping place, my grandma's.

I loved grandma, and I loved staying with her on her smallholding with chickens and goats and pigs. She grew vegetables and flowers which she sold by the bunch.

There were many happy, and funny, memories from those visits. One was frightening at the time. The lavatory was an antique, home-made affair in a wooden shed several yards away from the house. I hated using it, especially when it was dark. There were no electric lights to show the way, you had to grope your way there, scraping your knuckles on the house walls. The toilet was a bucket. Resting on the bucket was a board with a circular hole slightly smaller than the top of the bucket.

One dark night I just had to go. There was no choice, and no short cuts as there were sometimes, depending on the nature of the call.

I wasn't happy. There was no proper path, and a legacy of the animals' wanderings was often left around. It was with some relief that I eventually found the door, and with even more relief that I sat down. I usually sang, no doubt to hide my fear and keep away evil spirits, but there was no singing on this occasion - I was too frightened. I've always had a vivid imagination, but this was not imagined. I had company. I could hear someone scratching his way towards me. I leaned forward, listening intently - and felt a scratch on my bottom! "Help", I screamed and rushed out into the night.

Grandma came rushing to my aid. "Gran, Gran he's in the lavvy." Grandma kicked the door and demanded - "Come on out. Preying on children, you ought to be ashamed of yourself."

And then he emerged. A big black rooster climbed out of the bucket, opened his wings in defiance, took a swift look at Grandma on the warpath, jumped down and scuttled away.

There was no television for the masses in those days, and when rented radio became available we marvelled at it. I loved the variety of programmes and was allowed to sit up - if I had been good - to listen to Palm Court Hotel and Max Jaffa.

Saturday night was the time for a visit to the cinema, and we saved our money all week for this trip to the Astra cinema in Bradford's Wakefield Road, about three miles from home. A group of us walked together, the older children taking charge. We sang all the way there and back, walking in the road and hardly

17

ever meeting a vehicle. I enjoyed the walks nearly as much as the films, which were mainly Lassie, Old Mother Riley - oh how I loved Old Mother Riley - weepies, and musicals which were also a special favourite of mine.

Mother was a hardworking, proud housekeeper. The linoleum on the floor was polished until you could see your face in it, and the old furniture was brought to a similar glow. There was always a smell of polish in the house. The front room was out of bounds except for family visits and Christmas day.

The house had a cellar, a ground floor which had a tiny kitchen into which we all crowded, a first floor which had three bedrooms, and a second floor which had two attic bedrooms. As I grew older it was my job to scrub the wooden floors.

We slept several to a bed, topping and tailing they called it. A man's heavy overcoat acted as the bedspread, and bricks heated in the oven, and then wrapped in mother's old lisle stockings, acted as hot water bottles.

The cooker was part of an old range which had to be black-leaded every week, and it included a boiler to heat the water. A bright copper kettle was always singing happily on the fire, and a cup of tea always on offer to visiting family and friends.

The bath was a zinc tub in front of the fire. Seating space was at a premium, and a special treat in the winter was to be able to sit on top of the gas boiler.

Later we moved to a fairly new council estate in Boltby Lane, Buttershaw, and there we had the luxury to end all luxuries - two inside toilets and a bathroom.

I didn't cope too well at school. I was good at English but hopeless at maths. I had a happy-go-lucky, couldn't-care-less attitude towards school, and thought teachers were snobs. I enjoyed sport but was never quite good enough for the school teams.

I went to Usher Street Junior school, Bolling Grammar School for Girls, and Usher Street Secondary Modern School in Bradford - in that order.

I passed the eleven-plus examination to move from the Junior School to the Grammar School but that brought many problems. Mother was able to secure a grant for my uniform when I first started the Grammar School but there was no further grant when

I grew out of this, and I soon became conspicuous as the only girl in the school without a uniform.

All the time my mother wanted me to leave school as soon as possible so that I could bring another wage packet into the home, but we couldn't even afford for me to leave Grammar School because that would cost money we hadn't got. Having accepted a place at the Grammar School you were expected to stay there until you were sixteen to complete the course. If you left early you had to pay compensation of, I think, ten pounds.

At this time mother had been forced to give up work to look after my sister Beryl who had TB and we could not afford that ten pounds. Similarly, mum could not afford the little luxuries that seemed to be taken-for-granted necessities at the Grammar School - set square, hockey stick, ingredients for cookery lessons, and such like.

After missing more time off school when I dislocated my elbow, which made me an even worse attender than I had been before, the Education Authority transferred me to the Secondary Modern School, a move that pleased my family because it meant that I could leave school at fifteen. I was happy about the move, too, because it had been a miserable spell at the Grammar School.

There was, however, always the light relief of those weekend visits to the pictures and variety shows. I don't know how it happened, but I have also grown to like opera and ballet, something far removed from the culture of my working class background. I suppose it is a touch of class creeping out! I have never been to a live performance of either, however.

Over the years, I have also developed a love for reading. My favourite books are historical novels, Catherine Cookson's in particular, and, perhaps not surprisingly, I like medical stories! And romance. I am a romantic, really, because I like stories to have a happy ending.

I feared, however, that my leaving school would not have the happy ending I hoped for. Mother wanted me to work in the mill. I hated the idea and was determined that I never would. That stubborn streak was showing again.

2.

THE MILL - For a While

DESPITE the lack of money in the household we always had enough to eat. It was bread and jam for breakfast, and jam and bread for tea, every day, and always plum jam!

My mum was a marvel. She could conjure up a meal out of virtually nothing. Three pennyworth of bones made us soup for goodness knows how long. She was a fine cook and her baking was always especially tasty. Things were even tougher when she had to stop work to look after Beryl, and she was keener than ever for me to start work. Before that was possible, however, I did help her in many ways. I looked after the other children and it still brings a smile to my face when I recall taking my brother out.

I would run like the clappers down the cobbled streets and our John, just a few months old, would bob up and down in his pram, thoroughly enjoying himself. Trouble was that one of the wheels had the unfortunate habit of falling off every now and again, and John was in danger of being catapulted out. It became a fine work of art replacing that pram wheel, and off we would go again hell for leather down the street.

Another of my jobs was to tear the newspaper into strips for the lavvy. Some might say that the now defunct Daily Herald and the notorious News of the World were just right for toilet paper! When the paper was cut to the required size, you had to make a hole with scissors and thread string through the holes. You were posh if you had a nail in the lavvy to hang the paper on! We had to put it on the seat!

I didn't mind this job as it was the only time that I was able to read the newspapers. I was not supposed to read the papers, and I never did understand this newspaper ban, because my brother was allowed to read them to his heart's content. My mother and father told me I wasn't allowed to because I was a girl! I often wondered what dreadful influences they thought they were protecting me from. Mother certainly did not seem to want to protect me from working in the mill and there were far more evils there than in the newspapers, far more experience of 'real' life. When I did leave school soon after my fifteenth birthday, I stalled her immediate ambition by obtaining a general clerical job, but I lost that when I was off work for three months after injuring my back. When I had recovered she was soon pressing again for me to get a job at the mill because the family needed the money, and the pay for young girls was better in the mill than in the offices. I just did not want to work in a mill and that was that, so I managed to get another office job. I earned twenty-five shillings a week (£1.25) and paid most of it to my mother. I had five shillings a week pocket money and out of that I had to pay a penny a day in 'bus fares to work, so I walked to work to save the money to buy myself a second-hand bike for thirty shillings (£1.50).

Most of the other girls I knew worked in the mill, and it was considered a little *élite* to work in an office. Because of this, and the time I spent swimming, I did not mix with many other girls. I worked from 8.00 a.m. to 5.00 p.m. and, when I went home, some of the resentment at my working in an office seemed to reflect in the welcome I received: "Now our Hilda, you are not one of the office girls now; you have come home - scrub that floor." I had to do this every night, and I hated it. One night I revolted and said I was not going to do it. I was adamant. The old stubbornness was showing itself again. My father, who was now working nights, stopped away from work the following night to give me a good hiding because I was 'getting too big for my boots'.

I had not been working in the office long before my sister was taken ill again and, to boost the family's slender finances, I had to give way and get a job in the mill. Believe me, that was a real blow to my pride. I went into the weaving department, and it was terrible. It banged and crashed, and a woman had just been killed by a shuttle which had flown out of the loom. For two or three weeks everyone was talking about that poor woman; then she was forgotten. When I went home at nights I was deaf to every-thing but the banging and crashing that continued ringing in my head. It was horrific. I was a 'dropper', and I had to put little pins in the machines and drop them over each thread. I hated it.

A dropper's job was for someone with sharp eyesight and was always the lot of a teenager. Each thread was held in place by pins. There were spinners and weavers and twisters, whose task was to twist the wool into yards, and there were dyers. The part of the mill where I worked was hot and stuffy and I always went home parched. Up to this point I had never drunk tea or coffee, but when I returned home from work I always had a pot of tea to myself, much to the family's amusement. I told my stepfather's sister, Aunt Margaret, that I hated it, and she came to my rescue because she had a friend who ran a lingerie shop, and I was taken on as an assistant there. That move led to me owning my first-ever pair of pyjamas at the age of sixteen. It was my birthday and I was going youth hostelling. My boss said I could have anything in the shop as a birthday present so I chose a pair of pink pyjamas. Until that stage in my life, bedtime attire had been knickers and vest.

I loved to go walking and youth hostelling, alone and quite unafraid, to places like Holmfirth where the television series, 'Last of the Summer Wine' is filmed. The freedom I enjoyed then amazes me when I look back. I certainly would not let my kids walk across the moors unaccompanied now.

After I had worked in the shop for a while, there was renewed pressure for me to return to the mill. I had to give in, but this time I went into the spinning section which was nothing like so noisy. When I was spinning, great hunks of wool were thrown over a round piece of machinery and the end was pushed into a slot in another machine. I had to let the yarn run through my hands and take out all the knots. The yarn was rolled round huge cones. Several cones were threaded through more machinery and the weavers made beautiful lengths of material and tweeds. However beautiful the finished materials were I was not happy there.

After the initial training, my first day's pay was £1.1s.1d. compared with my previous wage of thirty shillings a week. That was in 1953.

About this time my thoughts turned to boys . . . before that I had been too busy. There was a girl with whom I had become friendly. Her name was Ginger Sutcliffe. Well, Dorothy, really.

She had everything - good looks, figure to match, and boy friends galore. She was a dance hostess, teaching people - usually men, of course - to dance. I was beginning to think there was something wrong with me. I had not even had one boyfriend. I was never asked out by boys. I think it was because I laughed too much. Probably the real reason was because I had not mixed with youngsters of my own age, whereas other girls went out in cliques to the fair and to dances.

Anyway at the time of our blossoming friendship, Ginger Sutcliffe was writing to a lad in the Royal Air Force, and I pinched a letter the boy had written to her, and wrote back myself. I wrote to this boy, Bernard, who was stationed at Binbrook. "If you are wondering why Dorothy hasn't written to you, it is because she lost her letter and I found it, and I am not quite sure who this Dorothy is," I lied.

Apparently Bernard was one of those fellows who had a big female following, and he passed my letter over to one of his barrack-room pals. "Girls write to me all the time. Here is one I have never even met. Do you want her?" he asked. It was Pat who took the letter. Pat Ellis.

I have never been sure if Pat was as desperate for a girl friend as I was for a boy friend, but he did write back and set in motion the chain of events which led to me becoming Mrs. Ellis.

3.

PAT AND MARRIAGE

WE HAD ARRANGED to meet in Bradford's Foster Square, I was to wear this particular dress and coat, and he was going to be carrying – a bicycle wheel!

This 'particular dress' was my first new dress . . . no, I tell a lie, my second new dress. The first was of white *crêpe* for my confirmation, and it cost fifteen shillings.

The one aimed at catching Pat's eye was an apple green shirt-waister. The coat was of bottle green, loose at the front with a half belt at the back, and bought in a sale for one pound. The 'New Look' length had just come into fashion; it was long, and I floated around like a ballerina.

It happened just as we had planned. It was easy to recognise Pat. There were not many men in RAF uniform wandering around Bradford carrying a bicycle wheel! He asked "Are you Hilda?" and I said "You must be Pat." We walked around Bradford, although it was late at night, and talked and talked. I was only seventeen and all the family were sitting waiting for me when I arrived home, all eager to know what he was like. I liked him – ooh, I did! It was love at first sight for me, and I have loved Pat dearly ever since. He was the first, and only, man in my life.

Although I had fallen head over heels in love, I doubted that he would write again after he had seen me. When we parted that night we just said we would write. It was up to him to make the first move and I was thrilled to bits when he wrote straight away. Soon we exchanged photographs. Later I plucked up courage to ask Pat if it had been love at first sight for him too, but it wasn't, he had to admit. He did not believe in it. "It just grew," he said. Everyone said I had fallen in love with the uniform, but I knew differently. It was the man himself. That was a lucky day for me, for Pat has proved to be the backbone of my life. He has shunned the limelight but has always been a great support, tender and caring.

Pat was twenty-one and a National Serviceman in the RAF stationed at Binbrook, in Lincolnshire. Despite the miles between us, our romance whizzed along. We wrote often and met when we could. I had a friend in Cleethorpes and visited her so that I was nearer to Pat and we could see each other more easily.

We wanted to get married right away, but my family wouldn't hear of it. My mum tried to split us up. She liked Pat all right but was worried about how she would cope without my money. I was earning seven or eight pounds a week then.

We became engaged on Pat's twenty second birthday and talked about getting married, but mother told me: "You can't get married until you are twenty one". So I became pregnant - deliberately. We planned it that way, otherwise they would not have allowed us to get married. Even so, my mother insisted: "You can't get married because I haven't any decent clothes to go to church in."

The reaction to my being pregnant? No outrage or anything like that. "Now Hilda, you have had a very heavy cold," said my dad. "Are you sure you're pregnant?" I was sure.

Strangely there was no expression of horror, no self-righteous indignation, mother gave me all kinds of pills and potions to take, but I flushed them all down the toilet.

Pat's parents were super. I was a bit in awe of them because they were better off than we were. His dad was the manager of a garage and, before that, both of them had been in service. Compared with us they were just like gentry. They had cups and saucers while we had only chipped cups. They had carpets on the floor, were never untidy, and had proper meals. At their house I had a bedroom to myself. I think they thought Pat was marrying beneath himself. Although they never suggested that in the way they treated me, I knew that I would not have been their choice.

The news of my pregnancy was revealed in October and the earliest we could get married was in January. We were married on January 8th 1955 - two days after my eighteenth birthday. But that expected baby never arrived, not as quickly as it should have done anyway, because Kathy did not appear on the scene until we had been married for eight months. No doubt step-father had convinced himself that he was right in his theory about the heavy cold. I knew differently.

I really believed that I was pregnant when I told my parents. In the event I could have got married in white, well almost, anyway. However I walked down the aisle at Shelf Parish Church, near Halifax, in a long pink dress and wearing a long pink veil. My sister Beryl and a friend, Sheila Naylor, were bridesmaids. No, not Ginger. She was a guest. She should really have been guest of honour for, without her, there would have been no wedding at all. She was still blissfully unaware of all that.

Pat's mother was a white haired lady who spoke quietly and adored her husband and family, the two boys, Pat and David, and Norma, who was Pat's half sister. Norma's mother had died and her father had remarried. Norma was married when I met Pat, and she lived in Kettering. David was at Manchester University where he subsequently gained his M.A. and went into the Church. He often came home at weekends and we had lots of fun together. He was a mimic and brought a great deal of laughter into the family.

Until he met me, Pat had been a keen cyclist, and pretty good at it too, winning a number of championships, but I must have slowed him down because he gave up serious cycling when we were married. Not, however, before I did a bit of cycling myself in those courtship days. I would borrow David's bike and ride around the countryside with Pat at weekends. In the summer we had picnics and spent a lot of our time out of doors. In the house we would help with the chores, and his mum would sometimes let me watch her bake in the hope, no doubt, that some of her skill would rub off on me. "Pat likes a pudding every day," she used to say.

It was a quiet, idyllic way of life. Some Sunday evenings Pat's dad took us into Skipton by car; other times we caught the train or bus at Hellifield.

There wasn't, however, much money to spend on pleasures. Pat had only one pound a week pocket money from his RAF National Service pay, and most of that was spent on fares travelling home.

Pat's father was a quiet man, and his son has taken after him. Mr Ellis owned one of the earliest Norton motor cycles, and sold his share in a family garage business to become chauffeur to Sir William Nicholson, of Hellifield, and he stayed with him until Sir William's death. He met Pat's mother there when she was a parlourmaid and secretary.

When Pat was eventually allowed to stay at our house, I had to pay mother ten shillings for the extra food, and I was still not excused my household chores. Every Sunday morning I had to do the family wash. Pat insisted on helping but, as the white clothes had to be boiled, the wash house was full of steam and we could hardly see each other.

We had no such things as washing machines. Heavily soiled clothes were put into a dolly tub and, after being knocked about in there for a long time, they were rinsed twice at the sink before being passed through the heavy wooden rollers of the mangle which Pat would turn while stealing a kiss and cuddle. My friends told me to refuse to do the work, but I never dared to do that although I often plotted to run away, without knowing where I would go. Pat always said things would get better.

During our courtship I still enjoyed swimming, and spent what spare time I had in the water. I cycled several miles to Manningham Park and, for three old pence, I could swim for as long as I liked in the pool there. After some success in long distance swimming races, however, I was allowed to swim in any of the local pools free of charge. Pat used to get bored watching me swim, up and down, back and forth, but his mother was convinced that it was seeing me half naked in a swimming costume that made him fancy me. Little did she know that Pat had seen more than just half of me naked! When preparing for a long swim I trained in the local canals whatever the weather. One weekend we took my brother Alan with us as I went on a training session. It was cold, oh, so cold, and Alan turned blue all over after just putting his big toe in the water and decided that a swim that day was not for him. I just plunged in and stayed swimming for nearly an hour until I was almost overcome by the cold and Pat had to pull me out of the water. I just stood there shivering and Pat had to pull off my swimsuit and towel me down before helping me into my tracksuit.

He was the perfect gentleman, and we never mentioned the incident until years afterwards!

Having started as a backmarker in the romance stakes, I certainly seemed to have made up for lost time. From never having had a boyfriend, I had met Pat and married within a year. On the train journey to our honeymoon in Scarborough, however, we began to wonder if we were really married and whether the ceremony conducted by the Rev. Samuel Boyland Brown had tied the knot officially, because we discovered a mistake in the marriage certificate. It was only that the vicar had wrongly described Pat's father's job but, in our youthful innocence, we were worried. Not sufficiently so to prevent us from continuing the journey and the honeymoon, mind you!

It was a 'weekends-only' marriage at first. Pat was still in the Air Force and, during the week, I lived with my mum and dad. At weekends we stayed at Pat's home where his mum had had a bedroom decorated for us. I was never completely at ease there – I think Pat's mum was always a little shocked by my description of my own home life – and, although his parents asked us to share their home, Pat discovered an unfurnished cottage in Binbrook that we could rent. He was always keen that we should have a place of our own and was very much against the idea of moving into RAF married quarters, even if that had been possible for a National Serviceman.

Kathleen Gail was just three weeks old when we moved into that cottage. She was born in the front room of my mother's home in the days before delivery in a well equipped maternity unit of a hospital became the normal practice. It was a difficult birth and, after requiring several stitches, I was not too well for a while afterwards, but Pat, as it turned out that he would always be in times of pain and illness, was gentle and kind, and waited on me hand and foot. He was on duty at Binbrook when the baby was born and when he asked for compassionate leave he was told emphatically: "No, women have babies all the time." His request was, however, granted by a higher ranking officer.

When he arrived in Bradford I felt surprisingly shy showing Pat our daughter. He was bursting with pride and almost glowed.

Pat's mum said the baby was the image of Pat; my mum said she was just like me!

4.

LINCOLNSHIRE - Our First Home

I AM SURE there are landmarks in everyone's life. One of mine was the day we moved into the cottage at Binbrook - our very first home together. I travelled from Bradford to Grimsby by train, Kathy in my arms. Pat met me at the station and hired a taxi for the hour-long ride to Binbrook. It was dark when we arrived at the cottage - No 7 in the middle of a row - but Pat had left a fire in the grate and it glowed red. The cottage was warm and welcoming. We both liked the oak beams and Pat promised he would oak stain and varnish them.

Kathy's pram was also travelling by train and on its own - but later. In it were all our wedding presents and bits and pieces of ornaments that I had collected together. It was a grey Silver Cross pram, a beautifully sprung baby carriage which cost twenty-nine pounds, brand new, and which was paid for weekly out of my earnings at the mill. It was several weeks before it arrived at Binbrook but everything was safe and intact. I was proud of that pram and, over the years, it became an old and trusted friend. I used it for all three of our children and it ended its days being used to take eggs from door to door when Pat started his own poultry farm.

It was the most natural thing in the world being a mother. I enjoyed it so much and it was lovely to have something that was mine. When we moved into the cottage at Binbrook we had very little else! Not even a bed. Our landlady lent us a mattress to sleep on. Pat was happy. It was our own little home.

The first night there we heard a strange noise. We sat up in bed and Pat said hurriedly: "I have been meaning to tell you - we are overrun with beetles!" He was right. He switched on the light and there were beetles scurrying everywhere. All efforts to get rid of them failed, and eventually we learned to live with them, just as the neighbours apparently had done for years.

One morning when Pat was late up I dashed downstairs to make his porridge but forgot to give his bowl a wipe before pouring the porridge into it. He grabbed the milk and sugar and tucked in, but raced off before he had finished. Another spoonful and he would have come face to face with two of the largest beetles you ever did see! The dishes were always checked carefully after this.

We went into Market Rasen to buy a bedroom suite and a cooker. We intended to buy two armchairs as well, but chose a settee instead so that we could sit together. Such bliss. We borrowed two chairs from the landlady, though, just to keep our options open!

Patricia was born at the cottage, just thirteen months after Kathy came into the world. I was so innocent, for five months I did not even know I was pregnant the second time around. I had breast fed Kathy, and everyone, including my mum and aunties, had assured me I would be 'safe' as it wasn't possible to become pregnant while you were breast feeding a baby. I never had a period after having Kathy, and began to put on weight. The neighbours begun to whisper that I looked pregnant and, just to silence their gossip, I went to the doctor – and he told me I was five months pregnant!

When we got over the shock, Pat and I were thrilled. I wanted a son, but there was no hint of feeling disappointed when another girl arrived. There was a shock, however, when we saw that her feet were badly deformed. Over a period of eight months, though, through the use of splints, her little feet were persuaded to come round to a normal position, and Pat and I were overjoyed when she learned to stand on her own two feet alone.

I well remember the day Patricia arrived on the scene. It was in the middle of September when, one day, I decided to wash all my blankets. It was a lovely day when I started but, by the time I had finished, it was raining, and the only way to dry the blankets was to drape them round the cottage. When Pat came home he thought he had stepped into a Chinese laundry. There were wet blankets everywhere. Needless to say, that was the day I started in labour. I had planned to have the baby at home and I had no blankets for the bed. It was terrible, but we came through.

Our marriage was a little turbulent early on because I was a bit of a 'devil'. I remember one incident in particular when I was very pregnant with Trish. I had been baking and was absolutely shattered. I had cleaned the house from top to bottom and had put a vase with roses on the table. I can picture it as if it were yesterday. The house looked really beautiful and there was a table stacked with cakes and pastries. Pat came in for lunch. We had our first course and I asked him to make the custard for the pudding. He replied: "No, I have been working all the morning."

I saw red. What did he think I had been doing? I asked him again, and again he said no. So I picked up the bowl of milk and poured it over his head. He sat there just like a goldfish blowing bubbles. I was ever so scared, and he turned round to hit me. He only just caught me a glancing blow on the arm, but I screeched: "You've hit me, you've hit me." I shot upstairs and did not come down until he had gone to work. Then I packed my bags and went home to mum.

When he went to strike me he knocked a bag of sugar all over everywhere and that was the final straw after all the work I had done that morning. A few days later I decided to return home, but I brought my sister with me as a bodyguard. She had to climb through the window to let me in and the first thing I saw was the frying pan still with the bag of sugar on it. Pat had been making his porridge in the morning and spooning the sugar out of the frying pan. He had eaten all the cakes. My bowl of roses was still on the table but the petals had been shed and were all in a heap on the table where he had left them, and the front door was locked.

When he returned from work he didn't know I was there, and he had this big surprise awaiting him. Don't forget I was well and truly pregnant. He was thrilled to see me, put his arms round me and said he would never hit me again - although he had not really hit me, and I had deserved all I got.

I had fits of pique but I couldn't stay mad for long. I can remember the first time we had an argument, but I cannot recall what it was about. The cottage had low beams, and I had gone all morning without talking to Pat. It sounds silly now, but I was rather proud of myself for that was an achievement for me, especially as I was dying to break the silence. Then, as I passed him, he pinched my bottom and made me jump so that I hit my head on the ceiling. By the time I came down I was laughing and, once I have started laughing, that is the end to my anger. I can't be cross any longer.

Now, with two babies, the little cottage seemed to shrink dramatically. Life was hectic with two babies born inside thirteen months. We called the second Patricia Dawn and soon she and Kathy were almost like twins. Our hands were full looking after the pair of them, but we decided to add a little more work by building our own house!

Before joining the RAF Pat had been an apprentice joiner, mainly to please his parents, but he did not want to continue in that trade when he left the RAF and returned to civvy street in 1956. Instead he took a job as a labourer on the RAF camp at Binbrook, and we stayed in our eleven-shillings-a-week cottage for another year.

We hankered after a place of our own and we spotted a plot of land on the outskirts of Binbrook. On it was a cottage and, after buying the land, Pat planned to renovate this cottage. That proved impossible because it had been condemned by the local authority and could not be lived in. So we bought a pre-fabricated bungalow, which was delivered in pieces, like a jig-saw puzzle, and we put it together ourselves, the two of us, with a little outside help.

Pat, always the handyman who has made me a super home wherever we have lived, dug out the footings. We employed professionals to lay the foundation and then we pieced together our new home. It was only when Pat put a chisel through his hand that we had to bring in more outside help until the injury had healed.

I never had any doubts that we could do it and, after several months' hard labour, our new home "Braysher Garth" was completed and the furniture was transported, from our first cottage home to the new bungalow, on the faithful pram! We had new linoleum for the floors, mum gave me her old curtains and Pat's mum gave us a rug. Pat put up shelves, made bedside cabinets and wooden toys for the children.

Building and moving into our new home did not occupy all our time. Not quite, anyway . . . and Garry Patrick, our third child and first boy, was born on December 15th 1959.

I was so excited to have a boy. Again I had the baby at home, while the two girls were looked after by a friend, and Pat took a couple of days off work to look after me. He coped well with all the washing and cleaning.

Among our happiest days were those early in our marriage that we spent at Binbrook. It was here that Pat turned to chicken farming, after an illness had forced him to give up his job on the RAF station.

Pat had always wanted to go into business on his own account and, with the aid of a bank overdraft, he started a poultry farm. The old cottage was still standing on our new plot of land - although it had been condemned there had been no instructions to knock it down - and this was turned into a poultry house. Upstairs we had chickens in deep litters, and downstairs we had them in battery cages.

Pat learned all about our new venture from reading books, and made the hen houses himself. This displeased the surgeon at Louth County Hospital who had been treating Pat, and didn't impress our building society manager who rejected our approach for a mortgage to enable us to start the business, but eventually the bank manager came to the rescue with overdraft facilities.

We bought chicks and ducklings and eggs and incubators, and my part in the enterprise was to take the surplus chicks to sell in Louth market. We hadn't a car, and neither of us could drive anyway, so I took a taxi into market each week until we became friendly with a man who offered to give me - and the chicks - a lift into Louth each week. Pat usually put a price on the chicks and, if they did not realise this in the auction, I was under instructions to bring them home. They usually were sold for the amount he wanted . . . until one fateful week. With the chicks still packed in their boxes, and with the rain pouring down, I struggled to Mercer Row where I usually met our friend at the end of his day in Louth. Because it was raining so hard, I took shelter in a doorway - a chemist's shop doorway.

A gale blew up sending the door crashing open and the boxes of chicks scattering into the chemist's shop, the boxes splitting open as they fell. Alarmed, the chicks made their bid for freedom, fluttering around and on to boxes of pills and bottles of medicines, and leaving their own indelible markings around the shop. It was like a bad dream – or a bizarre film – as we chased and finally caught them, to squeeze them all back into the boxes. Our friend arrived in the middle of the mêlée, and helped me put the boxes in the boot of the car. He told me not to worry.

But he didn't pick me up the following week!

We lived four miles from RAF Binbrook and received permission from the Commanding Officer to ply our chickens and eggs around the married quarters. Our transport was an old pram, the very one which had carried our three children around.

One morning the weather was uncertain so Pat decided to take a taxi to the camp. The taxi driver strapped the pram into the boot of the car and the eggs, in trays, were placed in the pram. They set off early and I called round to see a neighbour. The weather brightened up and the neighbour and I were sitting on a low garden wall when we heard the gate click and Pat, grinning widely, appeared round the corner.

"Guess what happened to me?" he burst out.

"The pram fell off the taxi and all the eggs spilled down the camp hill." I guessed wildly.

"Who told you?" Pat demanded. He wouldn't believe that I had just taken a shot in the dark.

He went on: "There we were, right at the top of the hill. There was a crash from behind and the pram was hurtling down the hill. I had to borrow a spade to shovel the smashed eggs off the road, watched by all the RAF families."

"Did you break all the eggs?"

"Well, not then. We picked the pram up and I strapped it back into the taxi, putting two undamaged trays of eggs back into the pram – only, on the very next corner we lost the lot again."

It was our first venture into the world of livestock. First chickens: Then dogs: Now rabbits.

As the price of foodstuff soared, however, we could not make this first business venture pay and we had to put it, and our coveted self-erected bungalow, up for sale.

The often zany relationship between Pat and me was highlighted by an incident at about this time. Pat was proud of the cages he had made to keep the chickens in and was scrubbing them out in preparation for the sale when someone called to see him. But while Pat had been working in the cages, I had locked him in and he couldn't get out. When the knock came at the door I had to say to the visitor: "Wait a minute, I'll go and let him out."

I called "Pat, I want you a minute", and he jumped out of the cage, went "cluck, cluck, cluck" and chased me all round the yard. The man who had come to call stood with his mouth open as Pat, with his wings down, chased me all round the yard without realising we had a visitor.

They were happy days. They were lovely. We had little money but we always had eggs and we always had chickens, so we could eat. We used to barter with friends, maybe, for a lettuce or some rhubarb. Yes, we were very happy.

The property was difficult to sell, but eventually Pat's mum and dad bought it. In the meantime, Pat spotted an advertisement for a gamekeeper and told me: "That's it – that's what I've always wanted to do." The job was at Brocklesby Park, near Grimsby, on the Earl of Yarborough's estate. A telephone call fixed up an interview but, when the day came, we were so hard up that we had only one gallon of petrol in the car, the very same car that we had bought when neither of us could drive.

It was a Vauxhall and cost us £75 – on hire-purchase – and while in our possession had never experienced the luxury of a full petrol tank. We bought it when I decided I was fed up with being cut off from the world at Binbrook and announced to all who would listen: "I want to learn to drive." On the day we went car hunting we had about ten pounds in our pockets and ten pounds in the bank. Then we bought the car as a means of getting home because we had missed the last 'bus! Pat told the salesman: "I will buy it if you will take us home."

We were pleased when we had both learned to drive. We both started to learn at the same time. I used my family allowance money to pay to go to a driving school for instruction. Pat had to rely on friends to teach him.

We took our first test in the same week. I remember my first test well. I wore my satin cheongsam dress, with fifteen inch slits up either thigh, my hair piled up in the fashionable bouffant style: I had carefully made up my face and applied my best perfume.

The test was in Grimsby and I knew I had blown it when the

examiner said turn left and I drove straight on. When we returned to the test centre he told me: "You look lovely. Your perfume is delightful - but your driving is atrocious." I had failed! But I passed at the second attempt.

It took Pat five tests to get through but, although I was the first to qualify to drive, Pat always had to put the car away. I was hopeless at reversing - especially into the garage.

But now we had the car and I could drive, so off we set for Brocklesby Park, expecting quite a lot from that gallon of petrol which had dwindled dramatically by the time we arrived because we lost the way. I was at the wheel, and drove in circles and the petrol indicator needle had been lodged on red a long time before we eventually arrived to meet the Earl of Yarborough.

A maid answered the door and we were asked to wait in a corridor before Pat was shown into a room to see the Earl.

Pat went in for the interview and I knelt down to play with a little dog. It rolled over for me to tickle its tummy and an elderly lady who came into the room asked: "Do you like animals?"

It wasn't until it was my turn for interview that I realised that had been my first introduction to Lady Yarborough. They took us to see the house where the gamekeeper lived and we couldn't believe it - it was just like a fairytale castle. Then his Lordship brought the interview to an end with a friendly: "We'll be in touch."

I had one final question, however. "Could you tell us where we can find the nearest garage?" His Lordship said to his assistant: "Take Ellis to the petrol pump and fill him up." It was the first time that the car had had a full belly in our ownership.

By the next post, Pat heard that he had got the job and we were on our way to a new chapter in our lives, a start to what was, I think, the happiest period of our married life.

5.

FOSTERING

IT WAS WHILE we were at Brocklesby - back in 1965 - that we started fostering children. Pat was away from the house a lot and I often craved for company. At this stage he would not let me go out to work. He was adamant that he was going to be the breadwinner. Full of chauvinistic ideals, he wanted his wife to be at home when he returned from work, meals at the ready.

How things have changed, and how well he has coped and adapted: not only looking after himself, but so often the kids and me as well. All this, however, was before the 'transformation'.

He had been brought up to believe that a woman's place was in the home, but I was beginning to feel that the world had something more to offer. We had three children and I had been advised by the doctor to have no more. I loved babies and happily would have increased my family. Sticking to the medical advice, however, ruled out this possibility, and Pat's insistence that I stayed at home meant no job for me other than housework. So my thoughts turned to fostering children and, although at first Pat didn't agree, he eventually changed his mind, I think because he saw that I was restless and he feared that I would insist on going out to work.

Our own children were ten, nine, and seven at the time, but I don't ever remember discussing with them my idea of introducing brothers and sisters into the house.

Brocklesby Park was the ideal place for children. There was plenty of space, open air, trees, lakes and parkland. It was lovely - a child's paradise. It didn't worry me that housework was a hard job in those days. No mod cons; not even mains electricity - but there was a generator to provide our electricity. What an annoying and frustrating piece of equipment that was. It was

37

always going wrong. First job in the morning was to set it going. Last job at night was to switch it off.

This was to lead to arguments. If when you got into bed and flicked down the light switch the light went out but the engine didn't slow down and stop, it meant that a light was switched on somewhere else in the house. The children slept in one wing of the house, up more than ninety steps of a spiral staircase; Pat and I were in another section. So you can imagine that neither of us was too keen to get out of bed and set off in search of the light that had been left on, and we used to race each other to bed, and the last one was the loser. Usually it was me, with a woman's guile, who won.

One night I recall I was the first in bed as usual, snuggling down and getting warm when Pat, just after climbing into bed, flicked down the light switch – and nothing happened. The dreaded engine rumbled on.

"Blast", or some similar word, came from his direction. We thought one of the children was still awake with the light on. We waited and waited for it to go off. Eventually Pat, unable to sleep, could stand it no longer. He thumped out of bed and was gone for about ten minutes before the engine died down. Soon afterwards he climbed back into bed and, ever the dutiful wife and aware that he would be cold, I snuggled up to keep him warm.

"You're wet," I shrieked.

"That's because it's raining," he replied.

The generator was in a building several yards away from the house and near the main road.

"You . . . you haven't been walking around outside with nothing on . . . ?"

"No, I put my wellies on!"

We laughed and laughed at the thought of what any passing motorists might have seen in their headlights. Oh, happy days.

One night, I remember, we heard a strange noise. We looked out of the window and there were frogs everywhere. Hundreds of them. Son Garry had had a tin bath full of frogs and had ignored our orders to replace them in the pond. They had all escaped and seemed to have been joined by their mates. So next day Garry was told firmly that the frogs must go. Next night we went to bed as usual: then the noise began. Rivet. Rivet. Rivet. The house was full of them. Frogs on the stairs, frogs in the kitchen, frogs in the bedrooms. Instead of taking them back to the pond Garry had taken the bathful down to the cellar, and there was no way the frogs intended to stay there. Next day Garry was carefully supervised as he took the frogs back to the pond.

We called the cellars the dungeons because they had windows with bars on them just above ground level. The kids would stand at the windows, peering through the bars at people who stopped on picnics or weekend rides and tell them in pitiful voices: "We've been locked in and haven't had anything to eat." The amazed passersby would hand them sweets.

In our home at Brocklesby Park there was a big kitchen, and the bathroom was downstairs, then you went up four stairs to the little sitting room. Above this were two bedrooms. Out of the living room there was a door which led to the gun-room. This was where His Lordship brought his shooting guests for a snack and drinks. It was my job to keep that room warm.

They called our house Newsham (pronounced Newsom). It was about three miles from the "Big House" and we were really on our own for much of the time. It was lovely.

Pat was enjoying the job, but I became increasingly restless because I wanted another baby. That was ruled out, but Pat eventually agreed that we could foster a child. We went to see the social services department in Grimsby only to be told that they did not have many babies for fostering. In any case they went only to 'special' people. The lady who interviewed us spoke to our children and asked if they wanted a baby in the home. They said they did but were not bothered whether it was a boy or a girl.

We didn't hear anything for a long time, and then we were asked to take in two boys from a children's home. The boys were aged eight and ten. The elder was really handsome but the other - Ken - wasn't at all attractive to look at. He had big teeth and straight hair but he appealed to me and tugged at my heartstrings when he said: "No one ever loves me: they always love my brother."

I still preferred to foster a baby but these boys needed a home for a short spell and, as our own children had gone to Bradford for a brief holiday, we had the space and time to look after the boys.

Phew, what a handful they turned out to be. First they flooded the bathroom and, as I was swilling the overflowing water out of the kitchen, I looked out of the window to discover that they had turned on the taps to the diesel tank. They had flooded the inside of the house with water and the outside with diesel fuel.

Our own children were usually lively but well behaved. I was strict with them, but firmness was always tempered with love. This pair from a broken home were something different. They came to us for several weekends but we were a bit taken aback by their mischievousness, and decided not to foster them permanently when asked to do so. We still had our hearts set on fostering a baby.

Then one day, in the middle of a family party, a lady knocked on the door and said: "Do you still want to foster a baby? If so, ring the office in the morning." I was so excited that I couldn't sleep that night.

Next day I went to fetch the baby, a boy. I had nothing to carry him in so took a drawer and laid it on the front seat of the car. I picked him up and gave him his feed. Nearby was a carrier bag and in it were three off-white nighties, nappies, and another bottle. That was all he had in the world.

He was six weeks old and his name was Stephen. His mother had been in hospital and the only reason for the fostering was that she was alone and without back-up. Her father had said she could stay at home only if she got rid of the baby. She already had a grown up son and daughter, and the father of Stephen was her regular boy-friend. The only solution to her dilemma was to put Stephen in care. Everyone was wonderful when I took him home and, for me, it was just like having my own baby. Friends found, or knitted, him clothes and my own children loved him from the start.

Stephen is still a loved, and loving, member of our family, although we were never able to adopt him because his mother never found herself quite able to agree to that; she was content to have him fostered, but not adopted. He has never wanted to find his own parents and, even when he was eighteen and I told him he was free to go and look for them, he replied simply and touchingly: "You are my parents."

In the early days I was terrified that Stephen's mother would change her mind and want him back. One day I received a call to take him into Grimsby to enable his mother to see him. I cried all the following night - but she only wanted to assure herself that he was all right, and she did not even recognise her own baby. He was four months old at the time. She was content when she saw how I loved her son. I have discovered that it is possible to love a foster child just as much as your own baby; in a mixed family you don't distinguish between the two.

On that visit Stephen's real mother and I sat side by side without knowing each other. We never met officially. Steve was in high spirits that day, giggling all the time. His mother held out her hand and touched him. She remarked: "What a lovely baby."

The following November we invited her to Stephen's Christening. She never replied. That Christmas, however, she sent him a toy engine and trucks. It was the last we heard of her but, silently, we have often thanked her for the gift of her son.

Mostly we fostered babies, and memories of many of those children come flitting back as I write: a family of three, including twins, came to us while their young mother had another baby girl which she named after me; a baby abandoned by its mother but reclaimed by its seaman father after I had nursed it night and day . . . the tears I cried at its departure; the child a mother reclaimed to avoid losing the milk token. Many we had for a few days, others for a few weeks.

During the summer I helped with the WRVS holiday scheme. Twins Susan and Julie were visitors each year, joined by their little sister when she was old enough. We would take in the misfits and homesick, and often there were as many as 20 of us sitting down for a meal at the extended kitchen table. Pat was fantastic with the kids. Evenings and weekends he took the older ones fishing, and walking in the woods, showing them wild flowers and fruits. He knew where to find a squirrel or a fox. He knew the woods so well, every tree and animal in it. He was happy.

It's not just carrying and giving birth that brings love; it's caring and looking after them; watching them grow, staying up at night to comfort them, sharing their joys and fears. All that brings love.

I have always told the children whom we fostered that, if

Pat and I had not done it, someone else would have done. They would not have been rejected.

After Stephen came David and Susan. It's always a worry, when you foster, that the children may be taken away at any time, but you mustn't let this cloud your thinking; you can't foster if you can't love, and accept that you may have to give them up at any time. You can't hold back; you can be hurt – but you can also receive tremendous rewards. In the eyes of the Authorities, I was now someone 'special', a willing recipient of children in need of love and a home.

Just to make sure that I had plenty to do, and to ensure that the kids had plenty of company of their own age, I also started a playgroup while at Brocklesby Park.

We fostered Stephen and David and Sue, and many more babies came and went, then, one day, Bill Adams, a senior social worker, told me about a baby in his care. A little boy. He had been in several foster homes already, but no-one wanted him permanently. The baby's problem? He was coloured. I didn't think of that as a problem, and welcomed another baby into my home. But Pat worried about what people would say, especially his employers, and I began to worry too. I needn't have done. He was a happy, chuckling baby, and everybody loved him. We called him Danny, and the vicar asked if that was because he had come to live in the Lion's den!

Danny was the perfect baby, forever happy and never any trouble, and he has grown up to be a good son, always a great help and comfort to Pat through my illness. Danny has always been ready to give a helping hand, run an errand or do any job, and we couldn't have chosen a more rewarding son. Now he is grown up he is popular with the girls because, they say, he looks like pop star Michael Jackson. Danny was the last of our foster children. The Social Services cried enough at four.

Before moving to Eastville we searched Lincolnshire for a large house with a large garden, and we made sure that we could take our foster children with us. They were transferred into the care of the Social Services Department in Skegness.

We were given permission to call them all Ellis to help them settle quickly into their new environment. They were, and are, Ellis's to us anyway.

Our Sue. Our David. Our Steve. Our Dan.

All have gone their separate ways now, except Stephen. He is the only one still at home, as keen as ever on the home comforts.

David and Susan are brother and sister. David ran away at the age of 14 to look for his real parents, but we are still good friends and he comes to see us when he can. He has settled in London with his girl friend, and is manager of a sex shop.

Susan left home at the age of 16 to take a job as a nanny in London. She is now living there with her boyfriend and their two chldren.

Danny isn't far away, and we still see a lot of him. He is living with his girlfriend's family in Spilsby.

Our other three children are married with families of their own - a boy and girl in each case.

Kathy, who started work as a cadet nurse in Louth, lives in Cleethorpes. Trish, after a brief, unsuccessful first marriage, met a Greek seaman while she was living in Immingham, and now they are living happily in Greece. Garry is close by in Spilsby.
We keep in touch now by letter, telephone, and visits.

In the days of Brocklesby Park, however, we were one big, happy, boisterous family.

We had to leave Newsham Lodge following the death of the Earl of Yarborough. Pat had been his 'little luxury' but the time came when there was no room for such luxuries.

For a spell, Pat worked for the Rabbit Society, exterminating rabbits, and then he was offered a job with the Forestry Commission. He decided, however, that he wanted to go it alone, and that was when we moved to Eastville to set up the kennels.

6.

THE BEST THING

THE BEST THING that ever happened to me was meeting my husband Pat. I tell him that nearly every day, but he just shrugs it off. Praising him is like pouring water on a duck's back. Many people hardly realise that I have a husband. He has always hated mixing and is something of a recluse. In the early days of our marriage he told me: "I would love to build a huge wall round the cottage and keep you all to myself."

The first time in recent years that he has accompanied me anywhere was to a Buckingham Palace garden party. But more of that later. It was lovely to see him out of his Wellingtons and overalls, and it is a family joke now that he is a snob and never accepts an invitation from anyone less than royalty: more recently he has been to Boston Borough Civic Dinner and my Freedom Ceremony.

I used to make the mistake of trying to change him, and I walked out on him in the early days because he made me mad, but I didn't stay away long and I was always the one who said 'sorry', although that does not necessarily mean that I accept the blame for starting all the tiffs! We have always had simple pleasures and, when the children were young, there was nothing we liked more than going on long family walks. Looking back I now realise that Pat's contentment to stay at home gave me the freedom and opportunities I would not otherwise have had.

I couldn't have gone out selling Tupperware, or even had foster children, if he had always wanted to be going out himself. I certainly couldn't have given anything like so many talks to raise money for my beloved DOCATEF. Also, if Pat had been an outgoing, socially-minded person, I am sure it would have caused friction when I was ill, or in hospital, and he had had to look after the children. He has always had a good relationship with the kids, and has

44

been kind to me and the family. He is not only my husband but also my best friend. At home we always had plenty to talk about.

Throughout my illness Pat's attitude to me has never changed. After treatment and surgery, I have felt undesirable, but he has always reassured me. "I don't love you for your face. I love the whole of you. It doesn't matter to me." "Well, it bloody well matters to me." I replied often, and it took me a long time to accept myself.

The worst time was when I had my maxillectomy. The radio-therapy was nothing, but when I had the major surgery to my face I was encased in what they call a halo; this was a plaster cast which fitted over my head. Wires came out of my mouth, my jaws were all wired, and I couldn't speak properly. I couldn't even have a drink without spilling it all over. After the wires had been removed, my mouth wouldn't open. The medical name of the condition is trismus. I could open my mouth wide enough to accept only a plain biscuit - not a double cream one, which I still can't eat.

I hated eating with other people and used to take my tray of food into the sitting room while the rest of the family were at the dining table. But Pat would not let me get away with that. He brought all the kids into the room with their trays and said: "You are not sitting here on your own." "I am. I am making a mess." I retorted. His attitude was: "If you want your food on a tray that is OK, but we will all sit with you and have our own trays." I gave in. "This is ridiculous, let's go into the dining room."

He would not let me get away with things like that, or hide away. He has had a tremendous amount to cope with, and I don't know anyone else who would have done it. I am full of admiration for him. If he had had lots of other activities and outside interests he might well have been resentful. I don't know how I could have coped without him. He was God-given. When I was waiting to go into hospital at Lincoln, I was afraid and depressed. I wanted to cry but my stubborness stopped me from doing that in front of anyone, even Pat. I used to turn over and cry in bed when I thought he had gone to sleep, but while I was crying I used to feel his arm come round me as if to say simply "I am here if you want me." There was one night when I was sobbing, and could not stop it when Garry burst into the room and shouted: "Dad, what are you doing to my mother? Leave her alone." It was then that I realised that I could not cry at night either because the kids were listening.

I am not afraid of dying but I dread the thought of leaving all my loved ones behind. As a nurse I have seen many patients die, and they have all had one thing in common after death - peace. Serenity in many cases after the pain. During my illness I have never thought that I was going to die. When you get a pain you think you must be dying, but then you think, "No, dying must be worse than this," and laugh it off. There were conflicting reactions from friends when they knew I had cancer. Those who came to see me after I had had radiotherapy treatment generally said: "You can hardly tell . . . if you pull your hair down on that side of your face." All, that is, except one particularly valued friend. She burst out "Oh, what a bloody mess," after she had taken a really close look. My reaction was one of relief. "Thank goodness someone is prepared to tell the truth," I thought. If that particular friend had reacted in any other way I should have been worried. It would have been alien to her character.

I was hurt by another friend. She was very dear to me and visited me virtually every day - until she knew I had cancer. Then she stopped. I know it was because she couldn't stand illness, but that really hurt.

At first we did not tell the kids I had cancer but one day after hearing the news myself, we were on the way home from hospital when we called into the village shop, where they had always been kind and helpful.

The couple who keep the shop said: "How did you get on?" Unthinking I burst out "Oh, I have got cancer." You could have heard a pin drop in the shop. There was a deathly hush, but Florence, the sister of the partnership, quickly recovered to say "I am sorry to hear that, is there anything I can do to help you?" I had found it so easy to tell her that I decided there and then to tell everyone who asked, and that is what I have done ever since.

The kids accepted it just as if I had measles - until Stephen, at the age of eight, discovered that he was born under the sign of Cancer. He was so upset, terrified in fact, because he thought it meant that he had cancer.

I did not know what to expect from radiotherapy treatment

but a friend, who had experienced it, told me: "There is no need to worry. It is no worse than having an X-ray." She told me what a super time she had had in hospital, how kind everyone had been, and after listening to her I was almost looking forward to going.

Before I had cancer I had been fascinated by the subject, and used to read everything about it I could get my hands on, but I couldn't imagine what I would do if I got it myself. I can remember my mother being so frightened of it, and she cried when the famous singer Kathleen Ferrier became a cancer victim.

What do I want my children to think about me? Simply that I loved them. I don't want their view of me to be completely taken over by this battle against cancer. I want them to see me as I am, scars and all, as an ordinary mum with all the failings of most human beings, but with a conscience and a great deal of love for them. I want them to realise what a super dad they have, and the burden that he has had to bear, although I am sure they know that already. I am not a goody-goody, and I would hate anyone to think that I am some kind of saint. I have had a lot of publicity but it is only illness that has attracted this attention and, if I could turn the clock back and make a choice, I would much rather have done without the illness and the publicity.

I don't think that having cancer is the most important thing that has happened to me, but it has enriched my life. I can't deny that. There is no conceit and I don't glory in it. Anyone can be unlucky enough to have cancer. I am lucky to have been given the character to have coped with it to some degree. All the attention that has been given to me and my fund can bring its problems but, if I were to allow it to go to my head, Pat would soon bring me down to earth with a bump. It's a family joke: "You are not in the Standard this week - we are not buying it."

There don't seem to have been many weeks when my photograph, and the now famous pirate's black patch where an eye once was, or items about my fund hasn't, appeared in the Standard which was so good in helping to launch the appeal. The newspaper writer Pat Ashberry is really the person I must thank most. She pitched the tone of her first article about Lyn Ellis just right, and it captured the public's imagination right away. Pat has grown to be a good friend and has continued to give the fund the best kind of exposure.

Soon after that issue rolled off the presses, the money started coming in. She has a special, sympathetic way of writing, and again I am lucky that Pat was the person I contacted about launching my appeal. I don't think I am particularly brave, although the suggestion is often made. This thing has happened to me and I am lucky to have been given the type of nature that has allowed me to cope. It has not been a vehicle simply to put the name of Lyn Ellis in the newspapers, and get her mentioned on radio and television. I would drop all that like a shot.

I say, always, and honestly believe, that I have not had cancer for nothing. I think I have had it to help others, and I believe that the other things in my life have happened to prepare me for this chance. For instance, the opportunity to sell Tupperware gave me the courage and confidence to speak to a roomful of complete strangers. Everything I have done has been geared to DOCATEF.

Husband Pat had known pain himself - and still does on occasions. That is apart from the pain of having to put up with me! He injured his back while we lived at Binbrook. He was cycling home from work one day when a woman, with an umbrella up to shield her from the pelting rain, stepped into the road without looking. Pat collided with her and that was the start of a long, painful spell for him. He had difficulty in walking. Attending the doctor's surgery for his weekly certificate was a nightmare. He could move only one foot slowly forward at a time, and had to hang on to a wall or hedge to climb the hill to the village.

At home he slept on a hard board. He spent ten days in Louth Hospital but only pain-killing drugs relieved the agony. Pat declined the chance of having surgery on his back at Sheffield because a friend had similar treatment and appeared to be worse after the operation than before it. Pat lost his job at RAF Binbrook because he was away from work for six months.

Pat's mum and dad were always helpful at this time. On their visits they brought food and love. Always they would write to warn us they were coming, and always would give their planned time of arrival. They were never late, never early. And that intrigued me, - just how they managed to arrive so punctually after a one hundred and thirty mile journey. After much quizzing, it was only years afterwards that they confessed to leaving with plenty of time in hand and then waiting a short distance from our house, maybe half an hour or so, so that they would arrive on time.

Against hospital advice, Pat signed himself off the sick list and, slowly and painfully, began to build huts and cages to start his dreamed-of poultry business. The first ducks he had were reared in a tin bath. We would push the furniture aside, spread out old newspapers and let the ducks wander around the lounge. They would line up like a column of soldiers as they walked round the room. Perhaps that was why they were called Khaki Campbells! Pat's eyes would light up as we watched them, and listened to the pitter of their feet on the paper.

One such night, as we sat on the settee, Pat wasn't feeling well, and he fell forward in a faint. Without thinking of his painful back, I pushed his head downwards between his knees. He was coming round and we both heard this click in his back. He sat upright for the first time in months then, gingerly, stood up. There was no pain - and he danced round the room. Then we danced together. Our doctor wouldn't believe it, and warned that the trouble could recur at any moment. The back is still tricky, but Pat has learned to heed the twinges and work within his capabilities, and he has enjoyed working for himself so that he can do jobs at his own pace. Even so, he must be regarded as a workaholic, refuses holidays and spends most of his time working.

As a teenager I always dreamed of getting married, and visiting relatives, especially my mum, at weekends, as I imagined married couples do. But it never worked out like that. My visits were on my own, or accompanied by the children but rarely by Pat. He didn't enjoy visiting. If the rest of the family went out, he used the opportunity to carry out repairs around the house, or do the decorating. It was always a family joke that I had left him too many jobs to do so that he had no time to seek anyone else's company. Truth was, he was happy on his own. We love each other, and trust each other.

Pat didn't enjoy shopping, visiting, or welcoming friends. He wanted me all to himself. I would sulk and cry, wheedle and tease, but I could never change him. I caused myself a great deal of unhappiness - and probably upset Pat too - until I realised that I would never change him.

As the children became older, I became involved in school activities, and became a Sunday School teacher for the very young, reading them stories from the Bible and helping them to draw pictures to take home. I took over the job as youth leader in the village, and organised dances and various other events to fulfil my yearning for company. Pat was always at home waiting for me.

7.

FIVE YEARS TO LIVE

IT'S NOT AN EVENT you're likely to forget – the day you are told that you have got cancer. It's like being sentenced to death without having committed a crime and, along with you, your whole family and loved ones are condemned to suffer because of a cruel quirk of fate.

Years on I can smile at the suggestion that I was given five years to live, and I can honestly claim that having cancer has enriched my life in many ways. I have made many friends and been on the receiving end of many kindnesses, expanded my horizons through starting the Detection of Cancer and Treatment Equipment Fund, been honoured by our civic leaders and become a household name in the locality, gained a lot of publicity and become instantly recognised. All because of the dreaded 'C'.

There must be more comfortable ways of achieving fame. All the pain, the suffering, the worry and heartache; all the laughter and tears, happiness and sadness, none of this has ever erased the memory of the day I was told I was yet another victim of that insidious disease.

To be told cancer had me within its evil malignant grasp was horrendous enough. Even more traumatic was the thought of telling my husband Pat. I was scared because I had cancer. It was taboo. I was scared, too, because of the upset and worry it would cause Pat.

The ritual had been the same every night I had stayed in hospital for tests and an exploratory operation on my troublesome bleeding nose. Pat and the four foster children came to see me, while daughter Tricia was usually out with her boyfriend, and son Garry was playing football. The younger children always looked immaculate and, after the greeting kisses and chat, they settled down to watch television as Pat and I exchanged news of the day, and he asked for instructions for the next day's meals and jobs to be done. The visiting hour flew by.

Each night, as we held hands, Pat would ask: "Has the doctor said anything yet?" I shook my head. I knew Pat was becoming anxious so, eventually, I made up my mind to ask the surgeon direct. My nose bleeds had stopped and I was beginning to feel better.

When Mr. Knowles, the surgeon, came in one afternoon, I blurted out: "I've got a lot of questions to ask you."

"In a minute," he replied quietly. "I have something to tell you."

Mr. Knowles was the ear nose and throat specialist and what he had to tell me was, simply, that I had cancer in my sinus – a condition that, if not treated, could spread.

I was terrified. I had never heard of anyone who had survived cancer.

He told me that I needed radiotherapy treatment at St. George's Hospital in Lincoln and, after that, further surgery.

"Oh my nose! They are not going to take my nose off. It's my best feature!" I had only heard of breast cancer, and they removed cancerous breasts.

Mr. Knowles told me not to worry about anything! Fantastic! Not to worry! He had just told me I had cancer – and not to worry! It was not until a long time afterwards that I realised what a difficult job he had telling a patient she had cancer and, as always, he was so very kind.

There was hope to cling to when he said: "You are going to be in my care for a long, long time." At least he didn't expect me to die straight away!

But what about telling Pat? That worried me enormously. So much so that I opted out and asked the sister to tell him. Cancer had killed Pat's mother and father. Waiting for visiting that night seemed like an eternity.

Two whole hours to wait and worry. I couldn't eat any supper.

The children came running in excitedly. One of the dogs had had puppies. They told me all about the new arrivals. In turn we kissed and cuddled and, gradually, the children settled down to watch television.

Pat, as planned, had been waylaid by sister. I looked at the children quietly absorbed in the programme. It struck me deeply how much they meant to me, and to Pat. How unkind life would be if they had to lose yet another set of parents.

I must not cry. They mustn't see me cry. I brushed away a stray tear. I was listening for the footsteps which last night made me so happy, but tonight . . . ?

Pat, a private but tender man, came into the room. There were tears in his eyes. He looked hurt and shocked. He walked towards me and tenderly put his arms around me. I could feel his heart thumping.

He looked at me and said simply "Oh, Lyn." I choked back the tears and pleaded with him: "Pat, help me. Please, please don't cry. You have to be strong for both of us. If you cry it will start me off and I'll never stop. Please help me."

He hugged me tight. We had the ward to ourselves. The other patients had gone home.

The children were oblivious to everything but their television programme, but whatever was happening at Crossroads Motel was nothing compared with the real life drama going on behind their backs. We looked at the kids, and Pat said: "You have to get better or else I shall lose the children. If I lose you and I lose the kids, I shall have nothing to live for."

From that moment we started to fight together. By the time Pat left the hospital that night we had started to sort things out in our minds, and were planning for my departure from the hospital the following day.

I asked Pat to tell other members of the family the worrying news. Later he told me of the reaction of his sister: "Oh, God, if that were me I would put my head in the gas oven," she had said.

It had been 1974 when I had eventually got to see Mr Knowles after a year of troublesome nosebleeds. Before then we had reached something of a crisis, Pat and I. He was fed up with me. I thought he was being unreasonable but, looking back now, I realise just how selfish I had become.

I was an area manager for Tupperware, and a good one too. I was in the top twenty for personal sales and unit achievements. I was ambitious and wanted to be Number One. I was out virtually every evening, often having two Tupperware parties a day.

Pat, meantime, was at home all day, working hard at the boarding kennels we owned. Our eldest daughter Kathy was a nursing cadet in Louth; second daughter Tricia was working at a lingerie factory; and our son Garry was still at school, as were our four permanent foster children, David, Susan, Stephen, and Danny.

Pat gave me the ultimatum: "You cut down on your parties, or I leave."

I didn't want to cut down. I enjoyed the job, the fun, and meeting people at the parties, and winning the prizes. But I didn't want Pat to leave. On top of this friction between Pat and me, my weight began to soar. I wasn't feeling too well and I ate and ate. I took to wearing long dresses and skirts in an attempt to hide my bulk.

I began to have nosebleeds too often for my liking. My G.P. seemed unperturbed. He told me this was common with women of my size and told me to lose weight, but I couldn't and, in the end, stopped going to the doctor.

The nose bleeds became more frequent. Pat continued to ask me to quit Tupperware. I still wanted to prove that I could make Number One saleswoman.

There was a tissue and toilet roll scarcity at the time. My friends helped out with stocks as the nose bleeds continued and, eventually and reluctantly, I had to go to the doctor again.

He sent me to the casualty department at Pilgrim Hospital in Boston, where I was treated and given an appointment to visit the Ear, Nose, and Throat clinic the following week – on Valentine's Day.

I didn't see the surgeon, but the doctor who cauterised my nose said that would solve my problem. I was really pleased, for ten minutes, then the bleeding started again.

My nose bleeds defied all attempts to stem them, and eventually I was admitted to hospital for examination under anaesthetic. I hadn't been able to do the parties and things were happier at home. The first steps towards learning I had cancer had been taken.

I quickly encountered my first problem. Boston General Hospital had no scales big enough to weigh me. They registered only eighteen stones. The admissions nurse estimated my weight at nineteen stones.

I was last on the list for theatre that day. When it was my turn a little Chinese nurse took me into a ward, pulled the curtains round a bed, pointed to a neat pile of garments and said "Undress completely, and put these on. When you are ready ring the bell." Then she left me.

I looked at the garments. I wasn't sure how to put on the gown but if I put it on to fasten at the back I couldn't make the strings reach, so I decided it must fasten at the front. I was dismayed at the large gap it left, but there was another puzzle - a square of cotton with long strings.

I couldn't imagine where it went but, after a lot of thought, I decided that it must go somewhere near my face as my operation was in that vicinity.

I put on the paper cap, pushing my long hair inside, then I tucked the piece of cotton under my chin and tied the long strings on top of my head. Then I clambered on top of the bed, rang the bell and, looking something like a Buddah, waited for the nurse to arrive.

She opened the curtains, let out a scream and ran away laughing. She gathered all the nurses in sight to come to look, and they could do little for laughing.

The white piece of cotton was, apparently, my fig leaf! And the gown should have fastened at the back. What had been intended as a day's stay started with a laugh, but ended with the news that I had to stay in hospital for a few days.

I left hospital *knowing* that I had cancer.

Before that I had only feared the worst - or had tried not to accept the possibilities. My nose had been bleeding night and day for a week before I saw Mr. Knowles. I was not losing a lot of blood, it was just a constant trickle, but it was getting me down.

On my first examination Mr. Knowles said he thought that there was a polyp there but said he wanted to examine me under anaesthetic.

When I went home I looked in the dictionary to see what polyp meant - it was a kind of tumour that could be benign or malignant - and it was then that I began to fear the worst. But when Mr. Knowles told me I had a tumour, he did not actually say: "Oh, you have cancer." There were always flimsy hopes, double meanings, to hang on to.

When he eventually told me I had a "cancerous condition which, if not treated, would spread ", I exclaimed "Oh, you mean I have got cancer."

At that time I had no experience of hospital life and was in awe of surgeons.

I was lucky in one respect: it was a very slow-growing tumour and Mr Knowles told me that I could have lived for several years without it being detected before it would have caused any serious problems.

The day I looked in the dictionary and thought: "Oh, God, I've got cancer," I told Pat and a friend - and they both laughed at me.

From that moment, however, I began to dread that I really had cancer. I did not know anyone who had survived the disease, and I read a great deal about it.

On an early examination, Mr Knowles traced his finger down my face, under my right eye, down the side of my nose to the top of my lip and said: "You are going to need really major surgery."

For all the discomfort I suffered I was not in pain, and normally you think that pain and cancer go hand in hand. The pain, cringing cruel pain, was to come later. When they started to make me better!

I used to make a joke of having nose ache because I had never heard of anyone having a pain in the nose. It was a dull ache, like toothache in my nose. We all thought it was funny.

When Mr. Knowles first broke the news to me, I did not ask a lot of questions, but I thought I was going to be all right in his care. You need someone you can really trust and, over the years, I have learned, time and time again, that I can do just that with Mr Knowles. He has been fantastic.

Strangely I did not have any sleepless nights - I have always been a good sleeper. That is probably one reason why I recover so well from operations. I sleep well, and I eat well. Mr. Knowles and I have a very good relationship - yet I would never dream of calling him anything other than Mr. Knowles. I am his longest patient, I think, and, of course, he has the right credentials. He is a Yorkshireman - or at least he once told me that his father's family came from Yorkshire.

Spring is my favourite time of the year and it seemed particularly poignant that I was not going to see my own garden blossom into summer as I said a tearful farewell to Pat when I was about to set out for Lincoln, and a spell of radiotherapy treatment at St. George's Hospital. We are not used to being apart and we don't like it. We just clung to each other until the ambulanceman interrupted our farewells with a curt: "Come on, I have got some more to pick up."

I was so full of tears I could not speak. They said I would be away for about five weeks - only thirty-five miles away from home, but a world apart from Pat because he could not afford to visit me.

As it turned out I was away for longer because of the various preparations I had to undergo.

When someone has breast cancer, for instance, they are able to mark the treatment spot with a pencil dye. Once the treatment has started you are not allowed to wash the affected area because it would blister. They did not want to put such a mark on my face, which was very nice of them. Also there was part of my face they did not want the rays to touch. For example, they wanted to protect my eyesight. They made a plaster of Paris mask for my face and, from this, they made a perspex mask.

I had to lie on what seemed like a dug-out canoe, and they screwed down the mask so that I could not move at all; this was to enable them to direct the rays exactly where they needed to.

The 'setting up' was terrifying, and the whole exercise was uncomfortable to say the least. Not only did I have to wear the mask, but also a lump of lead was placed in my mouth. They had to make it like a dental plate so that my tongue was not affected by the radiotherapy.

It took them about a week to prepare all these things. I couldn't wash my face for the seven weeks of the treatment, nor for three months afterwards. When I eventually went home Pat was terrified that I would forget and splash water on my face while

I was taking a bath or wash.　He used to mount guard to make sure that I didn't.

There was no pain attached to the treatment;　the ordeal was in the isolation.　Each session lasted no more than fifteen minutes but when I returned to the ward I was always tired.　I often said I felt like a slave being taken to the slaughter.　At that time I wore long dresses to try to hide my bulk and, once in the treatment room, I had to climb up three steps before lying on the table.　The long dresses made this difficult.　Then the technician fastened me down and left me all alone.　She said that if I was worried or frightened I simply had to lift up my arm and she would stop the machine.

Gradually all the noises around became familiar, and the experience became less of an ordeal each day.　The treatment was once a day, five days a week, Monday to Friday.　I was encouraged to go out of the hospital for a few hours when the treatment had finished and I was lucky in having a friend living in Lincoln, and I was able to visit her.

They were a mixed bag in the ward, some depressed and some pretending the whole thing was a big joke.　There was one woman who thought she was a cut above the rest of us, and she was always annoyed when I hung my huge knickers out to dry on her radiator!

The treatment was scheduled for no more than a fifteen-minute spell – of which only six minutes was radiation – on five days of each week over a period of five weeks, but I was there for seven weeks because of the time it took them to make my mask, and then the treatment was interrupted when I was ill with a virus.

I went into the treatment sessions with this advice from another patient: "When you lay there, start counting."　I took her advice and that helped to pass the time away as I became familiar with all that happened.　I really had no pain.　I couldn't feel a thing. It was just the sense of isolation that was the worst part.

In one respect I was lucky it was my face.　Imagine what it must be like for people with cancer on other parts of their body, not being able to wash for three months.　For me it was not too bad having only part of the face to leave 'unclean'.

The day I went to Lincoln our farewells had been hampered by the presence of a man from the Social Services, and I left Pat undergoing a means test to see if we qualified for any financial assistance to enable him to visit me. We couldn't afford for Pat to drive over to LIncoln, although I was able to get home at week-ends.

I was often tired after the treatment but you were discouraged from lying on your bed in the daytime. To liven up the proceedings one day, I did a 'streak' in the ward, but I was sitting down safely by the time the staff came to investigate the noise and commotion, and played the innocent when the inevitable question was put: "What me? No - I had my nightdress on - round my head."

I met Clara while I was in hospital in Lincoln. She was eighty-three and winning her fight against cancer to such good effect that she lived for several years longer. One day she asked me "Do you say your prayers?" I replied: "I used to do, Clara, but not any more. I have thought about it but I haven't said my prayers for such a long time. Why should God help me now? I would be using Him." She tut-tutted: "You naughty girl" - and off she went. That same day a curate visited the hospital and put the same question to me: "Do you say your prayers?" "No", I replied, "but you are the second person to ask me that today. I have gone such a long time without saying any prayers, I don't feel I can start again just because I am ill. That would be using God."

The curate replied: "You are a mother aren't you? If it were within your power you would do things the children asked for wouldn't you?"

"Of course I would".

"Well, God is your father, why don't you ask him?"

Clara came back into the room after the clergyman had left and I said: "Clara, I would like to say my prayers, but I don't know what to say." "Come on," said Clara, "the easiest way to tell you is to show you. Come here and kneel down."

So we knelt together at the side of the bed. First of all we said the Lord's Prayer, and then she went through the members of her family, and the poor and the sick and the lonely. After that I had the basis for my own prayers, but I still could not ask God to heal me.

I asked for serenity, and asked God to give me courage to accept the things I could not change. I have been given what I asked for but I realise that asking is a two-way thing. He can always say "No".

I believe in God and say my prayers every night now. Gradually I turned to prayer for healing. I had tried everything else and nothing seemed to be working so I have been to faith healers. I was not very impressed.

Had I not been a nurse I could perhaps have accepted divine healing more readily. I went to a service at the Pentecostal church in Skegness with a friend whose faith had to be seen to be believed. The preacher put his hands on me, blessed me, and said: "Sister, you are healed." As I returned to my seat my friend asked: "Do you feel better?" I didn't and I did not expect to, but she firmly believed that I would be dancing around the place immediately.

Then it was suggested that I should go to the healing services which have been held regularly at Boston Parish Church. I was told: "We have been saying prayers for you, why don't you come along?"

I dithered and dallied before making the telephone call to say "Yes." I was very self-conscious but the vicar, Canon Trevor Collins, was so kind and obviously pleased to see me. When he asked: "Are you coming out in the part of the service where we lay on the hands for healing?" I could still only say: "I don't know."

As the service progressed I looked across at the other people present and caught the eye of another cancer victim I knew, someone who had had her breast removed. She looked at me in return, and we went forward together.

Almost straight away after that service I was diagnosed as having a recurrence of cancer. But I did say that God can say "No" didn't I?

This, however, has not reduced my faith in God. The marvellous thing about Him is that He is always there. You can talk to Him wherever you are, and whatever language those around you are speaking.

When I went to visit my daughter in Greece and felt so horrible and everyone around me had a different way of talking, I could still speak to God in prayer.

I kept in touch with Clara, and called her mother because she mothered me in so many ways while we were together in hospital.

When she died, her family asked me to go to her funeral. It was not until I arrived at the church that I realised that she was a Mormon. She had never put her religious beliefs to me. We were of different faiths but we still believed in the same God.

I still ask God to be healed but I always know at the back of my mind that one day He is going to say "No" and it will be full stop . . . full stop.

Yes, I still ask to be healed. He heals others, so why not me?

Each time I have a new problem and go back into hospital I hope my fears are unfounded, but I think my prayers are answered in a way, because I appear to be given an inner strength to enable me to cope with whatever is thrown up. I will try anything to fight cancer.

Believing in God is part of my life now, like breathing, eating, sleeping. I speak to God and call Him Father and 'Jesus' Master.

During that stay in St. George's Hospital, I didn't have any mid-week visitors because Pat could not afford the cost of the journey, and Clara was always a big comfort. I still keep in touch with Clara's daughter, Mavis, and her brother Nobby. They are living reminders of how much I owe to her.

Pat came every Friday to take me home for the weekend, and he took me back to hospital every Monday morning.

Another patient at the hospital, Mrs. Bertha Hodges, lived at Mareham le Fen, and we took her home each Friday and collected her again on Monday. We were discharged the same day and promised to keep in touch, but within a month she had died.

I have had many operations and am restricted in many ways, but I am still alive and that is a miracle.

Miracles are engineered by God.

For a lot of my married life it has been a necessity for me to go to work. I have needed to do it, not only for the money, but also because I thrive on mixing with people. First there was the job of selling Tupperware. I became one of the best at that, and was promoted to area organiser. My secret ambition, however, had always been to be a nurse but, having contracted cancer, that dream appeared to have gone out of the window. I had made such a good recovery following my treatment at St. George's that the nursing ambition began to burn again so, after consulting Mr. Knowles, and knowing I had the full support of the family, I began to investigate the possibility of nursing work.

As I steadily got better I applied for many jobs, but I was always rejected when any prospective employer heard of my medical history - and I was always honest about that.

Eventually, I telephoned the Nursing Officer at Boston General Hospital and got an appointment. After discussions with Pat, I decided it would be easier for me to cope with a job if I plumped for becoming a nursing auxilliary, at least as a starting point. The Nursing Officer was extremely kind and I felt at ease talking to her. I told her about my ambition to be a nurse although I thought a nursing auxilliary was the best way for me to start. She had two vacancies, one full-time and one part-time. When I said I would like to apply for the full-time job, she advised that I try for the part-time one, and she helped me to fill in the application form. I had to have two references, one of which had to be from the surgeon who had been treating me. Within a week I had a call for another interview, and the Nursing Officer told me that Mr Knowles felt that I could tackle a full-time job. I was offered the job and the starting date was . . . April 1st! I was to start at the White House Hospital, Fishtoft.

I thanked the Nursing Officer for 'taking a chance' with me. She replied: "We take a chance with all our nurses and we seldom feel let down. We train young girls and, with many, as soon as they qualify, they marry and start a family."

I certainly was not planning to cut short work to have a family. Seven was enough! Pat was apprehensive but, as usual, supportive. The children were excited, and I increased their pocket money in return for their taking on extra jobs around the house.

After the excitement of that first day at the White House Hospital, where they catered for chest patients and infectious diseases, and after feeling straight away that I was doing something really worthwhile, I settled into the routine of work. A few months passed and the Nursing Officer called in at work to see me. She was pleased with the way I had fitted in, and asked if I had thought about training to become a State Enrolled Nurse. A new course was due to start in November.

I hadn't any 'O' Levels so that meant that before I could be accepted, I had to sit the G.N.C. examination. There were just two of us taking the exam. on that occasion, and the other was a girl not yet twenty! After completing the papers, we sat, fingers crossed, hoping and praying, as they were taken away to be marked. The young girl had asked if she could go first when one of the tutors came to tell us the results. I strained to listen to the conversation and just managed to catch: "I'm sorry dear, you did not pass this time. But you are young enough to get some 'O' levels and have another try."

The disappointed young girl departed but shouted "Good luck" as she went. The tutor joined me in the room and my thoughts must have come out aloud as I feared the worst because she smiled at me and said: "To the contrary, dear, you have passed."

I started to cry. She put her arm around me and said: "You should be smiling, not crying." I sobbed: "I'm very lucky. Only last year I had cancer and now suddenly things are running my way." One of the tutors disappeared and returned with a pot of tea. "I am sorry it is not something stronger," she said. My hand was shaking as I took the tea and said: "I bet I am the only one to pass the test who needed a cup of tea to get over the shock."

I would have loved to have studied to become a State Register-ed Nurse, but that course, at three years, was a year longer than the S.E.N. course and I did not feel that I could ask for even more support from the family than I would be asking already. In the early days of the course I had to say my prayers in the car because I knew that as soon as my head touched the pillow I would be asleep. My family was fantastic. My meals were always ready when I came in, and Pat always ensured that the car was in working order. Often there was studying to do at home after the forty-hour week. But if I hadn't grasped the nettle and taken the course then the opportunity would never have arisen again.

I started my S.E.N. course on November 2nd 1974, when the School of Nursing was at Boston General Hospital – I had reached the upper limit for acceptance. In the twelve-strong band of stud-ents there was another lady of my age, but the rest were just young-sters fresh out of school with their 'O' levels and C.S.E.'s. We two 'mature' students always sat together and we must have been the bane of the tutor's life; we always seemed to do the wrong thing and have the class in uproar, but we also had to work that little bit harder to keep pace with these bright youngsters. In some cases we were tackling subjects we had never done before. Our school days were long since gone.

Every three months I went to see Mr. Knowles at his clinic for a check-up, and twice I went into theatre for a biopsy. Every time I was given the all-clear as the report came back: "There is no evidence of malignant cells".

Mr. Knowles would push the report at me and say "Look, you know a bit about nursing now, read it for yourself." I always wanted to read it from my name downwards but all he was interested in was showing me the bottom of the report.

The S.E.N. course started with a month in school, with text books and practical training. I always volunteered to be the guinea-pig. I let the other students wash my hair, bandage me up . . . and I never learned properly how to do bandaging because I always volunteered to be the patient. Actually I was always taking the opportunity to sit down! Occasionally during that first month we went onto the wards; my first experience was on the men's surgical ward and it was really nice. I felt I was being a proper nurse at last.

Then came a three-month working spell on the wards, and I was horrified to discover that the time had arrived for me to give my first injection. The prospect scared and worried me. Every time there was an injection to be given, the confident young-sters would ask: "Can I give it?" I used to go into the sluice to clean bed pans, or went off to make beds - anything to avoid giving an injection. Then one day Sister took me into her office and reassured me that I was shaping up well as a trainee nurse, but she had noticed that I had not yet given an injection. "To tell you the truth," I confided, "I am scared and I don't want to give one." Sister wagged her finger and told me: "I have never heard of a qualified nurse who has not given an injection - you are going to give the next one."

Trouble was that I just did not feel that I could do it, and I begged Sister to allow me to take home a syringe so that I could practise. A puzzled sister asked how I was going to practise, and I replied that I wanted to draw up water into the syringe to make sure I could judge the correct dosage. She relented and let me take a syringe home. The children showed great interest when I took it out of my handbag and explained that I was hopeless at giving injections and would get the sack if I did not prove that I could do it. I said I needed a volunteer to practise on – and they all went quite white, but little Stephen, the whitest of them all, started to undo his jeans, and said: "Well, I don't want one, Mum, but if it will help you I will have one."

I cracked out laughing, and they realised I had been joking. I spent the rest of the evening pushing the needle into an orange by way of practice. It didn't improve my confidence. When I arrived at work next day, Sister said: "You are giving your injection today, aren't you?" I replied: "Yes, Sister", with no enthusiasm whatsoever. "The first one that comes along is yours then." After a while she sent for me. The task was to give a diabetic called Harold an insulin injection. Sister came into the clinical room to help me prepare my little tray . . . syringe, swabs and insulin.

I went up to Harold, but asked sister if I could take him to his bed and draw the curtains so that no one could watch me. She agreed, on condition that I left the curtains slightly open so that she could see me. Harold was sitting at the far end of the ward, puffing contentedly on his pipe. I said: "Come on, Harold, time for your injection" and to my horror he started to roll up his sleeve and said "Right Nurse, I'll have it there", prodding his arm with his finger. "No you won't Harold, you will come on to your bed," I insisted. "The other nurse gave me the injection while I sat here," he grumbled.

Harold couldn't see what all the fuss was about, and I didn't want to tell him it was my first attempt at an injection. He was determined he wasn't going to move, Sister was watching, and I had little choice. Harold continued puffing on his pipe, his sleeve was rolled up, and I thought: "Here goes."

I tore open the swab, and I must have rubbed his arm for about five minutes as I tried to put off the evil moment, and then plunged in the needle and emptied the syringe of insulin into his arm. What a relief! I felt his hand on my shoulder, and heard him say: "Eeh lass, that was the best injection I have ever had. You never know how long them young 'uns have been at it. Give me a mature nurse any time."

I felt ten feet tall as I walked back to Sister. This time the tray was rattling, not because of my nerves but because of my laughter. I was never afraid of giving an injection again. Mainly, however, I have been on the receiving end. I wish I had a pound for every jab I have had.

My nursing training continued and I volunteered to work on the gynaecological clinic where I worked with a surgeon who was a bit of a tartar. But if you stood your ground you could get along well with him. He was the only surgeon who took me to one side and warned me: "If you are going to work on my clinic I expect you to be discreet. I never want you to mention a patient by name, and if ever I hear that you have done so I will have you dismissed. Whatever goes on in this clinic, these patients come to me in confidence and I respect what they tell me." He made it perfectly clear that what went on in those four walls stayed confidential.

One day I was in attendance when he was doing a vaginal and rectal swab. I got confused and when he asked me which was which I said "I don't know." He shouted: "You are a bloody fool!" He apologised to the patient, explained that I was a 'bloody fool' and started all over again. This time he grabbed my wrist each time and said: "Vaginal - rectal, put it in the right one."

I finished my training and worked for two years at Boston General Hospital. I decided to move slightly nearer home after a severe winter. One morning, in particular, convinced me I could do with a shorter journey, when the road was blocked at nearby Sibsey. I stepped out of my car and my eyebrows and eye lashes froze to my face; I could neither move my car backwards nor forwards. I went to a bungalow, knocked on the door, and was greeted by a lady who exclaimed: "Oh, bless you, come in."

The sign outside said "Derwent Antiques". It was like stepping into another world. There was a huge table, highly polished; antique chairs; old fashioned fireplaces; and lots and lots of brass. It was beautiful - everything immaculate. And there was I thawing out all over the place. The lady just sat me on a chair in front of the fire, brought me tea and hot buttered toast, and said: "You don't remember me." I confessed I didn't, and she continued: "When I was in hospital to have my veins out, you were so kind to me and now I can repay you."

To cut down the travelling I took a job at The Gables Hospital, in Spilsby.

I had been at the Gables about a month when a circular came

round advertising a forthcoming lecture on cancer at Pilgrim Hospital. I applied for a study day so that I could attend, but the Nursing Officer said: "Oh no, not with your history." She relented when I said I would take a day off, and go anyway. I enjoyed the lecture, went home and, as I was cleaning my mouth, I thought I could feel a lump. I had not felt it before, and I was in the habit of examining myself carefully. I went through into the bedroom and told Pat: "I have found this lump" and made a joke of it because I had just come from a lecture on cancer. Next day I was aware that the lump was a reality. Three weeks passed and I knew that I had to do something about it, although I felt very well at the time. A visit to Mr Knowles resulted in a biopsy, a couple of days off work, and a week's wait for the result. I remember it was such a nice day – the kind that makes you glad to be alive.

As I stopped at the traffic lights in town, I spotted one of my old chums from that S.E.N. nursing course, a boy we called Johnboy. We wound down our respective car windows and chatted, oblivious to the hooting of impatient drivers around us. "How are you?" he asked. "I've never felt better," I shouted as I drove off to Pilgrim Hospital. As I made my way to Mr. Knowles's department, slightly late, I heard a nurse say: "She should have come today. Mr. Knowles wants to see her," telling her colleague to telephone to see if the missing patient was at home. The nurse looked up as I approached and said: "Oh, she is here." Immediately I began to panic, and thought something was wrong, but the nurse smiled and simply said: "I wondered where you were."

But there was another omen. I went to the waiting room and one of the usual perks of being a nurse was that you jumped the queue. But this time Mr. Knowles kept me waiting until he had seen everyone else. When we came face to face, he did not have to tell me what was wrong. His look told the story.

As I had been driving to Pilgrim Hospital I had happened to see my face in the car mirror and thought: "God, I'm lucky. I had all that treatment and you can't tell. My face is unblemished." That good-to-be-alive feeling evaporated rapidly as Mr. Knowles, unsmiling, said: "Lyn, I haven't got good news for you. The cancer is back and it is widespread. You are going to have to come in for surgery." He knew I was planning a holiday in Greece with my daughter Trish, and said: "I am sorry, your holiday is off."

8.

CANCER AGAIN

I picked up my handbag, and walked back to reception. The girls there could tell by my face that there was something seriously wrong. One asked: "What is the matter?"

I blurted out: "I have got cancer again," and burst into tears. "I just don't know how to tell Pat."

But I knew I had to tell him myself this time, because he always said he wished I had been the one to tell him before. That was my biggest worry. On the way home I had to stop the car because it was raining so hard: only it wasn't raining. It was me. There were floods of tears. For twenty minutes I sobbed my heart out. When I arrived home there was a car in the drive. Pat had a visitor; it was the social worker who kept in touch with us because of the children being fostered.

I was determined not to say anything to Pat in front of someone else, but I just blurted out: "I have got cancer again." as the social worker sipped her tea. You just couldn't believe the look on Pat's face. He never spoke, stormed out of the house and slammed the door.

I sat on the settee and had a little cry. I thought to myself: "He is mean, walking out on me like that." I was comforted by the social worker, but when she left I went to look for Pat and complained: "You are not fair to me, you know. It is me who is going to have the surgery, not you." He just put his arm around me and said: "I am sorry, Lyn. Why? Why should it happen again? You got over the other, you look smashing and everything is going fine for us." We just clung to each other. We both cried.

We were struggling to establish the kennels business at Eastville, and my money was vital to the family.

This was the big one. The operation that was to change

my life. The plan was to cut underneath my eye and down the side of my nose, through the top lip to take away one side of my cheek and jaw and palate. They were going to do a skin graft by taking a big square from the top of my leg to put in my mouth to promote the healing when they stitched me together again. The operation lasted five hours and twenty minutes.

All that was bad enough, but it wasn't my biggest worry. The night before the operation, Mr. Knowles came to me and said: "I am going to do a tracheotomy in the morning." That really worried me more than anything else - cut my throat and put a pipe in! Of course, had I thought, I could have worked out for myself the necessity of such an operation but it came as a shock to be told that I needed it.

All this was in July, five years after the first treatment. This was a very rare operation and Mr. Knowles carried it out with the assistance of Mr. Westmore and Mr. Glendinning. When they took me down to theatre the porters were joking about my weight, but, at fourteen stones, I was a shadow of my old self! Don't forget, I had 'weighed in' at an estimated nineteen stones five years earlier.

When I woke up I was in the intensive care unit. I had tubes just about everywhere, and my head was in a plaster cast - my halo, the only one I am ever likely to have!

One of my first thoughts was what has happened to my hair? It was waist long at the time, but sister had plaited it and I now looked like a Chinaman.

But what about my mouth? They had put in something that was like a piece of concrete. That is the only way I can describe it. It was just like concrete and there were wires sticking out of my mouth. It was to stop my mouth shrinking. Strangely, it did not make me feel as if I wanted to choke. My speech had gone anyway because of the tracheotomy, and, because of this, everyone seemed to think they had to shout at me. When I was given a board to write on, the first message I wrote - to all and sundry - was: "I am not deaf, or daft."

The inability to communicate was extremely frustrating. There was one hilarious example of this. In the intensive care unit you are comply naked, covered only by a sheet, and you can feel very vulnerable. I looked up after awakening one day to see an old nursing colleague, Paul, and he was telling the other nurses:

"The last time I saw Lyn was in the VD clinic." I wanted to shout out: "But I was a nurse working there, and not a patient." But all I could manage was silence. On another occasion, after drifting off to sleep, I woke up to find my own nursing officer holding my hand. I thought that was lovely. She really cared.

During this time I had no pain. I was still drugged, and it was more or less just discomfort. Generally I think I have a good pain threshold. I have learned to say: "Go away, pain." And it goes.

I would never deter friends from visiting me because I was in pain for I know that, when I become engrossed in conversation, the pain will go. I never thought to ask if there was any chance that I would not recover from this operation, and when I woke up I thought: "Well, I am here. I am still in the fight." I had never asked what the odds were but, having had the full amount of permitted radiation treatment on the previous occasion, surgery was the only answer this time.

I was in intensive care (which was ward 2C) for about five days, and then I went on to ward 2B, on the same floor, where I had a room of my own, and it was lovely. My friend Lyn, with whom I shared such fun in Nursing School, was working on intensive care. She was fantastic, and always came to spend some time with me before and after her duty spells. There was always someone I knew in the hospital popping in to see me.

I was in hospital about seven weeks that time.

After a few days Mr. Glendinning said that this 'piece of concrete' should come out. They took me down to the theatre on one occasion to clean my mouth and, afterwards, he said: "You can start taking this out every two days." I was being fed through a nasal tube and had a drip up. When I came out of intensive care I wanted to feed myself, and they brought this liquified 'gunge' and I said: "I am not having that. I am having proper food or nothing at all." It was, in fact, only liquified normal food, but I was not going to have a liquified diet come what may. I was determined to be as near normal as possible. I couldn't open my mouth wide, but could just about squeeze a plastic spoon between my lips, or push food through with my fingers.

Then came the problem of taking this concrete thing out of my mouth. Someone - I can't remember who, and I don't even know if it was true - said it had to be out for only twenty minutes before my mouth would start shrinking - only twenty minutes, then I had to get it back into a sore mouth. I just could not do it. It was a bit different from taking your false teeth out at night. It was like trying to fit a giant piece of the most complicated jigsaw in to place. It had to be placed so accurately or else it did not fit.

Moreover, the obturator - to give the concrete its proper name - had to be removed for hygienic reasons. My mouth was so tender, and I was repeatedly opening the stitches and making myself bleed. But they would not let me go home until I had mastered the manoeuvre. I don't think that I was a difficult patient but I just could not cope with this, and I was conscious that I was eventually taking up a bed when I could have gone home. I realised how lucky I was living in England and having the benefits of all the skills put at my disposal by the National Health Service.

Back home, Pat appeared to be coping well, taking things in his normally calm stride. The kids were older now, and I used to say to them: "Look after your Dad." Looking after Dad meant that they were looking after themselves as well.

At last I was able to go home, to become someone else Pat and the kids had to look after. I also had the regular help of the district nurse to cope with the problem of that damned obturator.

It never occured to me that I wasn't going to get better. It was just going to be a matter of time and I would go from strength to strength. Mental attitude is important, and I think I have been blessed with the right nature. There was one remaining obstacle to be overcome before I could leave hospital - the removal of the tracheotomy tube. I was worried and frightened about this. I feared that when it was taken out I would be gasping for breath. I did not know how I would cope with this. One Friday Mr. Knowles came round the ward and said: "I am going to take your tracheotomy tube out," and I said: "Oh, Mr. Knowles, not tonight. Please don't take it out tonight - leave it for another day." So he said: "All right, you can have it in for one more day." Next day, Mr. Knowles called into the hospital on the way to buy plants at a garden centre. I stalled for time again. I was scared. This gave me an extra hour's grace. "When I come back it is definitely coming out, so make up your mind while I am gone that you will have it out."

The hour passed, and the fear did not subside. I pleaded with Mr. Knowles, on his return, to leave it a little longer. But he said he would have at least to straighten out the knot that had come into the bandage. "Can I borrow your scissors?" he asked a nurse, and by that he had whipped out the tube in a twinkling. I immediately said: "Why did you leave it so long? Why didn't you take it out yesterday?" It was odd that I should have been scared of this, a minor matter, compared with the size of the operation. I have always had faith in Mr. Knowles, and have accepted drugs that kill the pain. I always say to myself: "That's his problem," and let him get on with it. When you've just had an operation they tend to over-sedate you. They give you the drugs on demand and you find the periods in between wanting painkillers becoming longer and longer until you settle down into a routine where one tablet every few hours keeps you reasonably comfortable. Certain drugs you find you can cope with quite well, others make you hallucinate and see little green men! I have rarely been without painkillers for years now.

At home I could not have managed without the District Nurse. Jan was absolutely fantastic. I had been told that I had to tolerate the 'concrete' for maybe two months and it had to be taken out and cleaned every day. What an ordeal it was putting it back in my mouth. I would sit and cry, or sit and swear. Or I would kick the dressing table. Or even pray.

Jan used to say: "Get on with it. The only way I can do it is to knock you unconscious and I am in no mood for fights today." I received no sympathy from her - or at least she showed no sympathy, quite deliberately, I know, because I had to do it myself and she was there simply as back-up in case anything went wrong. She really was hard to me - but in the nicest possible way!

When the prothesis was out, I could not speak. Jan had to dress my mouth and wounds. I had to tolerate that 'concrete' for several weeks. I have had a number of different ones since then. All are made of acrylic, it only feels like concrete! They waited for the wounds to heal and the skin to grow then they would make me another one, making an impression off this lump they pushed into my mouth.

After all the despair and problems and pain I had with this first prothesis, and despite the hours of help by technician Brian

Harris, I never really mastered the art of getting it out and putting it back in, so they made me another one with teeth on. Brian worked hard on this and, at last, he was able to say: "Come on, let's try it." It fitted perfectly just like a dental plate.

Brian is a little fellow and I was so excited I picked him up and squeezed him and twisted him round the room. There were tears in his eyes. I am not sure whether it was excitement - or pain caused by my bear-hug! The only drawback with this one was that it had great big teeth, and it made me feel like Penelope Keith. I had to wait a year before they could make me one with smaller teeth.

I receive free dental plates because I can't speak, eat, or drink without one. It is as essential to me as is a wooden leg to a limbless person.

Once I had mastered the art of manipulating the prothesis my recovery was surprisingly good, and my thoughts turned to going back to work. They were prompted particularly by regular visits to my home by my nursing officer who was a real pet. She was lovely, but due to retire in November, and it was her wish that I should be back at work by the time she left. Remember that it was in July that I underwent surgery, and I am sure it was the little incentive she dangled before me - a carrot for me to chase to speed me on the way to recovery.

So, on November 1st 1979, I returned to work at The Gables Hospital, in Spilsby, to discover that the Sister and staff had been informed that if I became tired, I had permission to make myself a cup of tea - something that is normally taboo for nurses on the ward - and merely talk to the patients.

Back to work - but that was not the end of my problems. They were shelved only briefly. The operation had resulted in problems with my right eye. Mr. Knowles had thought he had left enough orbital floor to support the eye, but it hadn't worked out that way. The eye began to drop, and I was suffering from double vision. I suffered from an infection of the eye, and so it was decided that I needed special glasses; one lens was clear, the other was not. People used to say to me: "Did you know one of the lenses is steamed up and the other isn't?"

I had been told that maybe plastic surgery would improve the appearance, and make the eye more presentable, so off I went to Moorfields Eye Hospital in London. However I didn't like the suggestion they made there that the best thing was to operate on my good eye and reduce it to the level of the bad one. "Rubbish" I remember saying in answer to that suggestion. "I have only one good eye and you are not going to mess about with that."

I was wearing a pink patch over my poorly eye at the time, but that became soiled and they gave me a black patch at Moorfields. That has become my trademark ever since and, for years now, I have stomped around looking like the Pirate of the Fens. In fact I think one ship visiting the port of Boston must have thought they were being raided by pirates on the day when my good friend, Councillor James Alcorn, arranged for me to go out on the pilot cutter to meet an incoming ship. With my black eye patch I must have looked every inch a pirate clambering up the rope ladder.

Anyway, I came back from Moorfields Hospital so bitterly disappointed, because I had gone with great expectations of having my face returned to something like normal. I have been told I wasn't bad looking once upon a time. The surgeon seemed cross with me but I insisted: "No, I don't want you to touch it. How would you feel if someone told you they couldn't do anything for your bad eye but they could do something with the good one!"

He said "I don't know how you feel. It means you are going to have to wear a patch for the rest of your life." That didn't worry me particularly; what did worry me was the thought of interference with my good eye, and the possibility of having no sight at all. In that fifteen-minute interview all my hopes were destroyed. I was so upset that, momentarily, it brought on one of those crazy suicidal feelings that I am sure many of the sanest people have had. A moment when the only answer seemed to be to end it all. Accompanied by a friend I went to the tube station to start the journey home and the black, black thought came into my mind: "I'll throw myself under the train when it comes."

My friend said nothing; she could see my disappointment and didn't know what to say. She didn't know what I was thinking. Suddenly the train came, and equally suddenly I was out of my black mood, and laughing - much to the surprise of my friend. I had thought that, if I did jump, what a hell of a mess I would make; there would be blood everywhere and, oh heck, somebody would have to clean it up. I started to chuckle and, once the funny side had taken control, I was all right. From pending doom to laughter in the space of seconds. That's nothing new for me. My sense of humour has often come to my rescue.

So it was back to work at The Gables Hospital - complete with the black patch covering my drooping right eye. My first job was to give a bed bath to a dear, demented old lady who couldn't even remember what day of the week it was. She asked what I had done to my eye, and she was very sympathetic when I said: "I fell off my bike." Just then Sister burst through the curtains and said: "Don't you believe it Nana. She came home drunk and her husband gave her a good hiding." With that the old lady threw up her arms, and said: "She's not going to wash me then. I don't want her near me." I was turfed out and sister had to give her her bath. Serve her right! That was in midweek. On Sunday I was on duty again when visitors came to the hospital and a lot of people were sitting around when old Nana, who was supposed not to remember a thing, piped up: "You see that nurse over there with a patch over her eye. She will tell you that she fell off her bike, but I know the real story, Sister told me. She came home drunk and her husband gave her a good hiding!"

The rest of the patients, all lovely old people, accepted my patch, and the staff were supportive and kind. I remember one day talking to Sister and saying that everyone had been so kind, and she replied: "We are a caring profession. If we can't care for each other what chance have the patients got?"

I did worry, however, that I was not pulling my weight. They were short staffed anyway and, if anyone was off ill, we were all expected to work a little harder to make up for it, but I wasn't able to do that and I felt I was putting extra work on to my colleagues. So I decided to give up nursing, and was advised to retire through ill health, rather than just resign, so that I could qualify for a National Health Service pension. After three months' attempted comeback, I had to quit, and I knew it was unlikely that I would work again.

Financially it was a blow, because the kennels were not bringing in a lot of money, and now I would have a small monthly payment - just enough to pay the mortgage - from the pension, rather than a weekly wage. There were six children at home then, but Tricia, seeking her independence, left home at this time to live in a flat.

The DOCATEF fund was getting into full swing. I had started it in the October of 1979 and, by the next February, £5,000 had been raised for the equipment Mr. Knowles wanted. In the following six weeks another £7,000 came flooding in to buy a gastroscope for Dr. Fairman.

My eye dropped further and further. I could see out of it only when I covered up the good eye; the two would not synchronise. they told me they couldn't do anything for the double vision, but they did offer to do a tarsorrhaphy - stitching the lids together on my bad eye. Cosmetically it would have looked better because now, when not covered by the famous patch, it bulged forward and did not look a pretty sight. The tear ducts had been damaged by the original radiotherapy when I first had cancer, and tears were forever rolling down my face. The tarsorrhaphy would have solved that problem and it would have ended the double vision, but Pat was dead against it. He had a theory that if the fresh air did not get to the eye it could be dangerous. He was against it when the reason for the operation was advanced as being cosmetic only. But gradually the pain became unbearable, and the eye became infected, so Pat changed his mind and I decided to ask for tarsorrhaphy.

In the first place, however, I thought I had better seek the advice of Mr. Knowles. Immediately he asked: "Have you considered having the eye removed? It will never be any good to you."

To lose the eye, surprisingly, was not as traumatic as I feared; it was a relief because it had begun to hurt so much. It was a relief too, discovering that there was no tumour in it. That was another operation under my belt, and another piece of my body with which I had started out in the world had been taken away. Now the black patch was a permanent feature of my appearance.

The relief from pain, however, was only shortlived and, because it became so persistent again, I was sent to London - King's College Hospital - for a brain scan. As a result they found more cancer in the ethmoid sinus, and part of the sphenoid sinus. The surgeon said I could stay in hospital and have the operation done, but that was moving too fast for me this time. I wanted to go home and talk it over with Pat, and not tell him bluntly over the telephone that I had cancer again. It was always in my mind that Pat's parents had both died from cancer, and how I had unintentionally bungled telling him on the first occasion.

We both knew, however, that there was no choice. It had to be done - so it was back to King's College for the operation, and there appeared to be no problem. They treated me very well and, during my time there, I became friendly with a young doctor, Dr. Tim Brocket and his wife, Yvonne. The doctor had lived in Boston as a young boy and had relatives in the town. Before I had the operation he and his wife invited me to their flat, and during my stay in hospital they did my washing. And even lost my knickers! The mystery of those missing knickers remained unsolved. They were just not there when the doctor returned the washing, and he was as amazed as anyone. "I remember them," he said. "They weren't even average size were they?"

By this time they had said I could go home - but there was no way I was travelling back to Boston without knickers! Pat had to send me a new supply. And he did - great big passion-killers which had been given for a Christmas present as a joke by one of the family pranksters.

It had been a tricky operation but the worst part of the ordeal was the journey home, not just because of the baggy knickers! A nurse accompanied me across London in a taxi, and put me on the train bound for Boston, with a change at Grantham en route. I was sick on the train, and there was a couple from Peterborough who were so kind and helped me to clean myself. I was really poorly but had to travel on my own. Over the loudspeaker the guard had asked if passengers would tell him of any special problems they might have, and, as he passed through the train, I plucked up courage to ask him for help with my luggage at Grantham. He said "Leave it with me, love." And he was as good as his word. As we approached Grantham he broadcast a special message to "Mrs P.N.Ellis, fresh out of hospital and not feeling very well. Stay where you are and I will personally carry your luggage." He did just that, and found a porter to help me on to the next train. That was the kind face of British Rail.

It took me a long time to recover from this operation, and there were regular checks at Boston's Pilgrim Hospital, but still the pain would not go away. I was convinced that the cancer had returned to my face. So off it was to London again, and another brain scan at King's College Hospital. I couldn't see the same surgeon this time, however, because he had suffered a stroke. I was told there was no return of the cancer to my face and, I suppose because I seemed so disbelieving while in London, I was sent a copy of the pathologist's report to prove it. I knew how I felt, however, and that was poorly, very poorly.

When I was sent back to King's College Hospital for more examinations and tests they decided to do a routine chest x-ray. Earlier I had been advised that the next port of call for a tumour of the kind I had could be on the lung, but I never gave that a second thought. It was in my face where the pain was, and I became very impatient with the young radiographer who insisted on taking a whole series of x-rays. I knew I had not moved and I thought she was incompetent and stupid. I took the papers back to the clinic where a panel of doctors reviewed the case. Eventually I was told: "There is nothing wrong with your head or your face, but there is a little spot on your x-rays. Will you have another one taken, please?" As I took the card I thought "Stupid girl, I knew she was incompetent." Then, as I went back to the X-ray department, it occured to me to read the card and I noted it said: "Query lesion third right rib." My reaction was: "Oh God, they have seen something and not even told me."

The radiographer was really nice this time and, after the doctors had taken a look at the new x-rays, I was told there was a suspicious-looking spot on my lung. It was Bank Holiday time, and the thoracic specialist had left early for the holiday. After they had contacted him by telephone, I was advised to go home as there was no immediate danger. I was even allowed to go to Greece to visit my daughter Tricia and family, but I was on my own and miserable, worrying about whatever it was on my lung.

I was a misery during that holiday, the first one I had had in Greece with my daughter. By that time I had heard about laser treatment for cancer patients and, when I went back to London, I asked if I could have the operation by laser, but I was told it wasn't possible and it had to be by traditional surgery. I was also told: "This is the most painful part of the body to have surgery, and the spot is only tiny so it is up to you whether you have it or not. It could be a peanut . . . it could be anything."

Knowing what I had been told about the possibility of lung cancer, however, and knowing too that I would never be comfortable with myself, always suspecting there was something on my lung, I decided on the thoracotomy. This meant a cut right down my back, round the waist and under the breast, easing ribs to one side to get at the lung. They removed a tumour. It was the size of a little finger nail, and it was malignant.

I was in pain, excruciating pain, and I was terribly unhappy during the recovery period after the operation. There wasn't a sister on the ward, and the charge nurse was on holiday. I didn't get on at all well with the staff nurses. The painkillers they gave me were very effective for a short spell, but they wouldn't give me any more, or anything different, when the pain returned. I had to resort to crying and rocking the bed when visitors were present to provoke them into giving me more painkillers. It wasn't difficult to cry. The misery and the pain brought that on all the time.

The nurses could have asked a doctor to review my painkilling doses, but they never did, and I requested to be transferred to Boston. On reflection of course, they were only doing their job and following orders. They said I was too ill to move. Then they said I was too ill to sit in a car, and they couldn't pay for an ambulance, so I would have to make the best of it and stay there. I was so unhappy that I sought the help of the hospital Social Worker. She was dubious about telephoning Pilgrim Hospital, and doubtful whether they would accept me in any case, but eventually she gave way and made the call. She returned to say: "They will welcome you back with open arms, but you still can't have an ambulance and you are too poorly to travel by car." I was insistent and asked the Social Worker to explore other ways of getting me back to my beloved Lincolnshire. Eventually it was arranged that I would travel back to Boston by Red Cross ambulance and the Boston Committee for Cancer Relief would foot the bill.

It was a bad experience, that operation, the worst I have ever had. The surgeon was right about it being the most painful operation possible. The pain really got to me.

Another problem transpired. The stitches they had used internally, had, I still insist, been the non-dissolving type and this led to all sorts of recovery problems. It was a long, slow, painful process. As usual they were super to me at Pilgrim Hospital, and made sure I was not in undue pain. I stayed there for about three weeks, but it took months for me to recover from that operation. A sad and painful experience. Maybe I was caught between two different ways of life - the slow, caring way of Lincolnshire, and the fast-moving, seemingly tough way they do things in London. Give me Boston any day.

This was the operation that gave me the worst pain I have ever had but, with the tumour turning out to be malignant, I am pleased I had it done.

On top of the cancer - as if that were not enough to cope with - another crippling complaint crept in almost unnoticed: Arthritis. One morning I awakened to find my hands all knotted up. They were painful and I could not move them. I could not dress myself, and I could not feed myself. Luckily tablets have kept it at bay since then.

9.

LASERS:
AND MORE HOSPITALS

TO TRAVEL TO Southampton and back to my home at Eastville is a journey of some 410 miles; it is one that I have made a few times now in my fight against cancer.

The connection was made as the result of an article in the Daily Express. I didn't spot it myself - we only read The Sun at our house then - but a friend did, and she telephoned to tell me about it.

There was, she said, this new drug, followed by laser surgery, to fight cancer. The drug was administered by syringe into a vein in the arm and, as it circulated round the body, it clung to the malignant cells, by-passing healthy cells.

A new vapour laser, when switched on, would shine on the cancer cells which could easily be eradicated by the laser.

"Send me the cutting, please," I asked. I took it with me on my next check-up date. The surgeon mentioned in the article was a Mr. Carruth, a pioneer in laser surgery at Southampton. Mr. Knowles showed a lot of interest.

A few months later I was invited to Boston's Pilgrim Hospital to see a laser in action. I had been involved, through the DOCATEF appeal, in raising £33,000 for a carbon dioxide laser. The technician told me all about it. There were three kinds of laser available, he said: one was capable of removing tatoos and tumours from the skin; the carbon dioxide laser that was being demonstrated was capable of removing oral tumours, and could be used in gynae-cological surgery, removing tumours on the cervix (neck of the womb) in out patients. The patient could have the operation, have a cup of tea, and then go home. The third one he told me about later.

It all sounded so simple. I wanted to know more. The laser

gives a beam of concentrated light and the surgeon shines it on the malignant area. While ridding the body of the cancer cells the laser would also seal off the vein ends. There would be minimal loss of blood and less chance of the cancer cells spreading through the circulation of the blood. At the same time the nerve ends would be sealed, thus eliminating pain.

I asked the surgeon present whether they were going to illustrate the use of the laser, and on what kind of patient. He looked at me in horror and said: "I can't operate on a patient. I shall have to go on a course under Mr. Carruth at Southampton to learn the skills. I'm not ready to operate on a patient yet."

But there we were all gowned and masked waiting for a demonstration of the magical new laser. There was a pause, and someone produced a tomato. With due ceremony it was placed on a stool. The technician, using a biro, drew a small circle on the tomato, the laser was switched on and the beam aimed at the marked spot. There was a sizzling sound and a puff of smoke. The laser had cut round the circle and left the remainder of the tomato intact. I was very impressed and determined that DOCATEF would raise the money for a laser of this type. I also said the fund would pay the maintenance for the first five years and running costs for the first two years. It's no good buying an expensive piece of equipment without making sure that there is enough money to keep it working, and without having the staff capable of using it to its full potential.

After the demonstration we retired for a cup of tea and the technician explained about the third type of laser, still in the experimental stage, used in conjunction with a dye drug.

It was the very thing mentioned in that article in the Daily Express. It was funny how Mr. Carruth and that laser kept cropping up. And so it was on one of my many visits to see Mr. Knowles following a bout of particularly bad pain, that, after examining me, he sat back, deep in thought, and finally said: "Would you be prepared to make the journey to Southampton to see Mr. Carruth?"

I was on the way to see the great man himself – but not without the help of my dear friend Bill, who had come to my rescue so many times driving me all over for key appointments. I cannot say how much I value his help and friendship, and that of our travelling companions, friend Ruth and Auntie Milly.

Ruth became a good friend when we were both selling Tupperware, and Milly is her Auntie. Bill Eason is their friend and he first offered to drive me to a hospital appointment when he heard how Ruth was planning to accompany me to London by bus. Auntie Milly is a Margaret Rutherford look-alike, and all three have been superb friends. Having them with me, the serious connotations of cancer have been forgotten and it has been a real laugh-along as we have driven from consultation to operation and back again. In the quieter moments Bill's Jim Reeves' tapes have soothed our journey.

So it was on that first trip to Southampton. There was a scare on our arrival. No-one on reception knew of our appointment. What a relief when it was sorted out! When I was called into the clinic a tall gentleman smiled and offered me a chair, and I asked: "Are you *the* Mr. Carruth?" "Yes," he said: "Why?" "I am just wary of imitations." I said.

He was reading my notes, and he talked about my fund. I told him that I had heard about him and read about his work, and he invited me to read the paper he had done on laser treatment. He showed me into an empty room where I could read quietly. I read it over and over again and made mental notes so that I could tell Mr. Knowles about it.

To have this treatment you first had to be injected with the drug H. P. D. which, over a period of four days, circulated round your body and clung to the malignant cells, making them luminous, and ignoring the healthy cells. The laser was used to burn off those malignant cells. I noted that I would need dark glasses as I would become sensitive to light; my skin would also become sensitive and burn in daylight. I'd need gloves and socks. I could not then remember the drug, but I got the procedure well into my head.

Mr. Carruth examined my face, then asked: "Do you want the treatment?" I was eager to have it. Mr. Carruth explained his difficulties. First there was the problem of getting a supply of the drug which was manufactured in America and Japan. And he was still waiting to get his own laser. He talked of the side-effects, and the allergy to sunlight and daylight. It seemed a small price to pay for the hope of a cure.

There was a long wait at home after that consultation with Mr. Carruth. Each morning I searched the mail for a letter with a Southampton postmark. When it didn't arrive I became depressed, and more poorly. I wrote to Mr. Carruth and a week later I received a reply. He had access to a laser in London and could treat me the following week. He would give me the drug in Southampton and I would have to travel to London for the surgery.

I waited until the weekend, but still the admission letter had not arrived so, in desperation, I rang the hospital in Southampton, but it was not until the Sunday morning that I received the return call saying that I was expected there before 11.30 a.m. the following day! The next few hours were hectic, but we were all set for the off by 6.00 a.m. on Monday morning, Bill driving, Auntie Milly sitting alongside him, and me enjoying the roomy comfort of the back seat.

On arrival Mr. Carruth examined me and reported that the tumour had grown little over the past two months. He planned to give me the H. P. D. by injection into a vein and then operate by laser to remove as much of the tumour as possible. Then I would go to King's College for follow-up laser treatment. I knew the treatment had begun in earnest when they pulled the curtains over the window of my small ward. I was no longer to be exposed to the daylight or the glare of the sun. Mr. Carruth had no difficulty in finding a vein and inserting the butterfly needle. The bung was removed from the short tube attached to the butterfly needle and some of my blood spurted out. "B positive," I cracked. "B messy," replied Mr. Carruth as he wiped his hands.

After administering the drug, he explained: "You will have to sit still now for two hours and your pulse will be recorded every fifteen minutes." I felt nothing from the injection, which was a relief, and after two hours the needle was removed. The staff were really kind and our Susan rang to say that she would be coming to see me the next day and would be bringing her baby for me to see for the first time. I was still thinking of our conversation when the ward telephone rang, and it was Sue's brother, David. I could hardly believe it. He promised to try to visit me in King's College Hospital on Thursday. Susan and David had been two of our foster-children.

That evening I had to draw back the curtains for a little fresh air; I don't like being closed in. But I had to close them again before I went to sleep as the night nurse reminded me that daylight began just before 4.00 a.m. At pill time I had one Diconal and one Voltarol, and a Corsodyl mouthwash.

So Monday was over, and it had all gone smoothly. I woke up once or twice but had a fairly good night, and so it was into Tuesday. I dread waking up in the mornings. My right cheek, eye socket, and side of my nose start to hurt and burn. I said "Yes, please" eagerly when the kindly nurse offered me a Diconal. I had my Voltarol at the same time, when she also brought me a mouthwash. I feel better when I am dressed and the Diconal eases the pain greatly. I am allowed them on request but try to keep the use of them to a minimum. It was a great temptation to draw back the curtains and open the window for a gulp of fresh air. Instead I put on the small light. Breakfast over, I was sent for an X-ray. I was told to strip to the waist and put on a gown. The lady repeated: "It fastens at the back!" She must have heard about me!

Back to the ward and hardly time to settle down to knitting when Susan arrived with daughter Kerry and her friend. Kerry is a pretty little girl and I was pleased Sue was able to come and show her off to me. Kerry created mayhem with the toys in the playroom but soon she was tired and the ever-thoughtful staff moved a cot into my ward so that she could take a nap. Sue and I, and Sue's friend Charmine, talked and talked until tiredness gradually came over me and, once they had left, I fell sound asleep. I awakened to Sister coming into my room with the news that I was to have the laser operation the next day, and on Thursday they had booked a car to take me to London for the other laser treatment. But there was no room for me to stay at King's and I would have to return to Southampton that night.

Mr. Carruth came to see me and chuckled to see me cuddling a koala bear. He said: "I'll have a good scrape round tomorrow," indicating my face. "I expect it will be a bit sore and painful afterwards." He joked about taking me to London in his old car and, with a flourish, he brought out the MOT certificate which it had passed that morning. He told me his car was twelve years old and maybe this showed a little of what kind of a man he is . . . content with his old car, devoted to his work, and happy to get on with it in a quiet and unassuming manner.

All the day's talking had brought on the pain again, and I had to have another Diconal. After supper I wrote to Sue asking her to let her brother David know that I was not staying at King's after all. I telephoned a couple of friends, brought my diary up to date, and rang husband Pat. At midnight I needed another Diconal, but then fell off into such a sound sleep that I did not wake until late next morning. The staff nurse came in with the anaesthetist who asked if I had had any problems in the past. I showed him the backs of my hands, where most of the veins had closed up, and asked if I could wear my obturator as far as the anaesthetic room. He patted my hand and agreed.

When they left I decided to have another sleep. I knew I was last on the list, and was surprised when the staff nurse returned and asked me to wash in readiness for my pre-med.

"So soon? Why?" "You are having an oral pre-med and they take longer to work," she said. I had twenty minutes for a shower and a visit to the chapel for my prayers. On a wall straight ahead was the figure of Jesus. The marks made by the nails at His crucifixion were bigger than any I had ever seen. I just had to look up and gaze. As I did so I remembered the time at school prayers when I was reprimanded for turning my face and eyes upwards. I had tried to explain that I was 'Looking up towards Jesus' but the head teacher had dismissed me from assembly. I had felt humiliated and puzzled. As I said my prayers this time, I asked for serenity.

Back in the ward I was given a tablet which, I was told, was Valium, and then waited to be taken into the theatre. I was still wearing my prosthesis as two porters, accompanied by a staff nurse, wheeled me there. The anaesthetist checked the backs of my hands and decided to opt for a vein at my right elbow. He inserted a butterfly needle, and I removed the prosthesis. For a few seconds I waited and then, feeling drowsy, I said "Goodbye".

I woke up in the recovery room. As I was wheeled back to my ward I felt very tired and wanted only to sleep. I kept waking up and drifting back to sleep. Once when I complained about the pain I was given 75 mg of Pethidine. The next time I asked for my usual Diconal. It worked wonders.

A nurse said my brother had telephoned, and would ring again next day. Mr. Carruth came in to tell me that he was 'fantastically pleased' with the operation; it had not been as serious as he had feared.   Afterwards I was not sure, in my dazed state, whether I had dreamed his visit.

At 8.45 p.m. Pat rang.   He was worried because he had not heard from me.   I was surprised that it was so late.   Next day I met Jack.   He was the man who was going to take me to King's College Hospital in London.   He never offered to carry my bag, and I struggled to keep up with him as he raced along the corridor. At the car he asked if I knew the way.   I replied: "You must be joking."   He got out of the car and disappeared for fifteen minutes. When he had returned he said: "I have another woman to pick up in Winchester.   I don't usually do long runs.   Some of the drivers refuse to go out of town, but it's all in the day's work, isn't it?"

I wore my dark glasses, cotton gloves and socks, a long sleeved blouse, and trews to protect my skin from the daylight.

Jack soon told me about his medical history.   He was sixty-five and had a pacemaker for his heart.   "Before that my pulse dropped to thirty-five," he chuckled.   "Have you had many operations?"

"Thirty two," I replied.

"Oh my Gawd," said Jack.   "You look better than any cancer patient I have ever seen, and I've picked up a few since I started this job in February.   I'm sixty-five you know, retired from Telecom."

We picked up the other patient in Winchester.   She walked with the help of two sticks.   Jack asked this lady's sister for directions to the hospital.   She advised: "Make for Clapham railway station - the hospital's just opposite."   Jack spoke to our new passenger.   "You been before, have you?"

"Aye," she replied, "many times."

"Good," said Jack, "You can show me the way."

As we sped towards London, it soon became obvious that neither had a clue about the direction we should take.   I swear we went round in circles, and stopping to ask pedestrians did not seem to help.

My appointment was at 1.00 p.m. and I was becoming anxious as the clock ticked round to 12.45 p.m. before, at last, Jack discovered the way to our companion's hospital - which was different from my destination.

"Your man will just have to wait," he said to me.

Eventually we found our way with the help of a hospital van driver. To my horror I realised that no-one had told me exactly where to go. We went to the transport office and I explained to a lady who I was and why I was there. She continued talking into her telephone and ignored me. So we went to look elsewhere. On a reception desk there were three ladies laughing their heads off. They were in a world of their own. Each time one spoke, they went off into fits of laughter again. Eventually the oldest of the three pulled herself together, made a telephone call, and directed me to where I wanted to go. Jack was worried about his car, and I told him to meet me at 4.00 p.m. I felt a bit like Judy Garland travelling down the Green Lane in the Wizard of Oz following the orange lines on the floor as I had been directed. I walked through a door marked 'Enquiries'. A nice-looking young man smiled and looked up. "I'm Mrs. Ellis and I have been sent from Southampton for laser surgery," I explained.

He closed the book in his hands and grinned: "I'm a patient myself. A girl keeps coming in and asking if I am all right. She'll be back again soon."

I rang a bell on the door. "It doesn't work," said the young man. I walked up and down the corridor. Eventually a staff nurse came. She was expecting me. I felt miserable, and worried that I was not going to have a general anaesthetic, but the nurse said not to worry because I wouldn't feel a thing. As I walked down the corridor with the nurse, a man approached. It was Mr. Carruth. I couldn't believe it. "Are you going to do it?" I asked and, when he replied "Yes", all my fears left me.

The treatment took just over one and a half hours, and Mr. Carruth was delighted with the result. He told me so and said he was sure he had killed 99.9 per cent of the tumour. It could grow again, but, if it did, he could easily control it. For the first time in eleven years I believed I could be cured.

Back in the transport office Jack was waiting. The nurse handed him my bag, but he ignored it and I took it myself. He hadn't found directions for the return journey, so it was pot luck again, and sometimes we went round roundabouts twice. But eventually we made it back to Southampton. After eating my supper that night I returned to the hospital chapel and, head bowed, I prayed. I prayed for a complete recovery. Next morning I was in a mess.

My face had swollen and it ached badly. I had to rest repeatedly as I packed my things. I had great difficulty in eating anything. I thanked the nurses for all their many kindnesses and prepared to drive back to Lincolnshire, all those miles away. Back to my beloved family and friends and in the care of those dear, dear, friends, Auntie Milly and Bill . . . No need to carry my own case with Bill around. No worries over the drive home. No fears about their kindness and consideration. I was in good company, and I needed to be just then.

Even with a mask on, my face felt hot and tight, my lips were swollen and my eye began to close with puffiness. I felt poorly and my voice came out only as a croak. We stopped at Peterborough for a snack, and I telephoned Pilgrim Hospital. They suggested I went to hospital in Peterborough, but I preferred to get back to Boston to complete my recovery in comfort.

While I was in Pilgrim Hospital this time, in January, 1985, I received many get-well cards, and I asked the nurses to fix them on the wall for me, in an arc and facing me. It looked like a rainbow. I told everyone it was my rainbow, and beyond it the pot of gold was a new healthy me. Garry, my son, wrote me this poem and called it *My Rainbow*:

You are my rainbow. A colour in every dream.
An arc of wonderful laughter, your grass is always green.
Your eyes light up the morning, like the sky so blue,
My world that keeps revolving, my one and only you.

Red is for the blushing of your tender cheek.
While orange is the sweetness I'll cherish week by week.
Green is for the emerald, a very precious stone,
That twinkles like a star at night and lights
our way back home.

Yellow is your sunshine with rays of love, and warm,
I always see my rainbow at the end of every storm.
Violet's for the flower, a small and fragile thing,
Which constantly reminds me of all the joy you bring.

Indigo's the mystery to what its colour may conceal.
The mystery of your thoughtfulness? But even that's
for real.
The shades denote devotion like a living story told.
I am happy with my rainbow, you can keep your pot of gold.

Around this time I broke into verse myself with this little effort:

The Surgeon Came

The surgeon came, his face looked sad.
I feared the worst, his news was bad.
He told me straight "You've got a cancer."
My mouth dried up, I could not answer.

At first I found I couldn't cope.
I lost the will to live and hope.
My husband said: "You must attack
This awful curse and fight it back."

I knew deep down that he was right,
So with his help I learned to fight.
We took each day, just one by one,
And climbed the hurdles as they'd come.

The surgeon came, his face aglow,
He said: "I think you'd like to know
After all the problems you've endured
You're free at last, you've won, You're cured."

On that journey home from Southampton I thought I had taken every precaution to protect my skin from the sunlight, I was draped in clothes and looked like someone from the Klu Klux Klan. I was conscious of passers-by peering into the car whenever we had to stop. Bill said he would get me a Sheik's outfit if ever we had to repeat the trip. Even so, by the time I reached Pilgrim Hospital my face was badly swollen and I had to spend some time in a darkened room. It was not long, however, before I was home and eventually I seemed to have made a good recovery.

I think I am more or less a happy-go-lucky person. I feel that, if I had been encouraged to study more as a child I could have had a much wider knowledge and done more for my own children, but it is only as I have grown older that I have realised this. I could have pushed them more. Before I learned to drive I had a terrible inferiority complex. I thought everyone was better than me, but that changed when I learned to drive. It was a time when there were not so many women drivers as there are today. Passing my test gave me loads of confidence and, since then, I

1. *My mum and step-father.*

2. *A reminder of my early days in Bradford. I am pictured here with my mother, step-father, brother and sisters.*

3. *The first photograph that I sent to Pat at the start of our love-match.*

4. *The first photograph that Pat sent to me.*

5. *Young love, Pat and I on the day we became engaged.*

6. *One of the few photographs we had taken on our wedding-day.*

7. *Me as a young mum, with babies Trish and Kathy.*

8. and 9. *Pat and I on the 50 mile Kennedy Memorial Walk which was organised from Louth when we lived at Binbrook, and Newsham Lodge our home at Brocklesby Park.*

10. *All the family. From the left: Garry, Sue, Trish, Danny, Kathy, Steve, and David.*

11. *Party time for the children, nephews and neices, and any of the children we happened to be fostering at the time.*

12. *Nurses - all newly qualified S.E.N.s. "That's me in the middle."*

13. *Mastering the technique of giving an injection.*

14. *An autograph from Member of Parliament, Austin Mitchell, a former presenter with Yorkshire Television.*

15. *Me in special glasses to hide the effects of surgery on my right eye.*

16. *Pictured with the children of Conway school whose efforts gave DOCATEF its first msjor-push.*

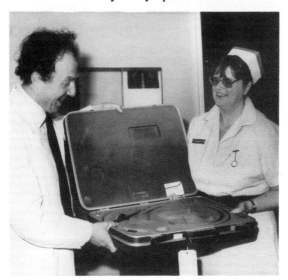

17. *The first piece of equipment paid for by DOCATEF, and I was so pleased to hand the laryngoscope to Mr. Knowles.*

18. *Phew! - That's hard work. The concert organised by Sandicliffe of Boston was another DOCATEF fund raiser.*

19. *Staff at Mackay's shop in Strait Bargate, Boston, have always been excellent supporters of DOCATEF.*

20. Ride him cowboy! Former mayor of Boston, Councillor Bob Marriott, and I try out two of the horses that were involved in one of DOCATEF's sponsored rides. Just after this photograph was taken the mayor fell off.

21. Me again - this time with Joanne Skinner, a regular fund raiser on our sponsored pony rides.

22. *Turning back the clock. Patch or no patch, I managed to return to my old love of swimming to take part in a sponsored swim at Boston that raised £400.*

23. *A lady to whom I owe so much - Eirwen Thompson - who has driven me thousands of miles in the cause of DOCATEF, often with her husband as navigator. Before Eirwen came on the scene I was very grateful to Sue Garner for driving me all over the place.*

24. The fund raisers come in all shapes and sizes. Circus artistes Val and Rex Halgarth organised a circus especially for DOCATEF.

25. Photographed with a good friend from the Lincolnshire Free Press, *columnist Sheila Robson who is also a member of the DOCATEF committee.*

26. DOCATEF Committee members watch me receive cheques from Francis Mountain of Quarrington.

27. More equipment for Pilgrim Hospital - this time for bone-marrow transplants.

28. *A start to my public recognition.* This was the time I was voted the Lincolnshire Standard's *Woman of the Year.* On the left is former Standard editor George Wheatman, and on the right their reporter Pat Ashberry. Also in the photograph are former Mayor and Mayoress of Boston, Councillor John Wright and his wife Marjorie.

E^{II}R

The Lord Chamberlain is
commanded by Her Majesty to invite

Mr and Mrs P. N. Ellis

to a Garden Party at Buckingham Palace
on Wednesday, 13th July, 1983 from 4 to 6 p.m.

Morning Dress, Uniform or Lounge Suit

29. *The Palace invitation.*

30. *Receiving the Civic award from the Mayor of Boston of the time, Councillor Cyril Fovargue.*

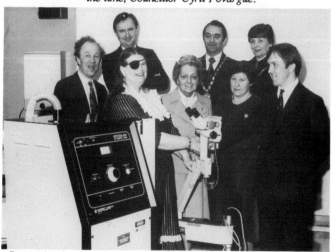

31. *Presenting laser equipment to Pilgrim Hospital. Also in the photograph, from left to right: Mr. Knowles, Dr. Fairman, Mrs. Babs Hall, (formerly the fund's treasurer), Cllr. Keith Lancaster and Mrs. Lancaster, Mrs. Noreen Evison (DOCATEF secretary), and Mr. Westmore.*

32. *Me again - with plenty to smile about.*

have been a much happier person. I am placid now, and completely relaxed. At least that's my opinion. I am sure Pat and the kids sometimes think differently.

I don't think people are nicer, or kinder, to me because I have cancer but the fund has certainly opened doors and given me access to people I would not otherwise have met. Sometimes I think I have too much of a conscience and worry if I think I have done something wrong or, perhaps, unintentionally upset someone. Life must be easier for people without these fears.

The worst time was when I had the maxillectomy. The radio-therapy was nothing, but when I had the surgery I was in what they called a halo. It was a plaster cast that came down my face and I had three wires out of my mouth, my jaw was all wired and I couldn't speak. I am not frightened of dying, but what I don't like is the thought of leaving everybody I love.

As a nurse every patient I have seen who has died has been peaceful, and the serenity has been lovely. Serenity after pain in many cases. Once you are dead, you are dead - but your soul goes on. I have never thought that I was going to die. When you get a pain you think: "This must be it." But then it comes to you that dying must be worse than this, and you laugh it off.

Why did I want to write a book? I thought it might be of interest to people even before I had cancer. People quickly forget how we lived forty, thirty, or even twenty years ago, and I thought it might be an interesting reminder of those days through relating what my life was like in my early years. Now that I have had cancer I hope my story will be of some encouragement and solace to anyone else who has the same misfortune of becoming a cancer victim.

I hope that there is no conceit, and I don't glory in the publicity I have attracted. Anyone can be unlucky enough to have cancer. Each and every one will handle it in a different manner. It has its problems having become some sort of local personality, but my family would never allow me to become big-headed. They would soon bring me down to size.

This is not a book about a saint. The first time I spoke to Pat Ashberry of the Lincolnshire Standard, when I first sought publicity for my fund-raising plan, I insisted that I didn't want anything printing that suggested that I was a 'goody-goody.'

I am no better than anyone else. I am not specially good nor specially brave, but I am probably lucky to be gifted with the type of nature that has allowed me to cope. Given the chance I would take thirteen years back, and be 'ordinary'. It has not been a vehicle to take Lyn Ellis into the public eye; I would drop all that in exchange for good health. I always say, and honestly believe, that I have not had cancer for nothing. I think I have had it to help others. I think it happened that I did my Tupperware selling which gave me the courage and confidence to sell a product and to speak to a rooom full of strangers as preparation for launching my DOCATEF project. Everything I have done has worked towards it.

10.

How DOCATEF Began

HOW DO YOU REWARD men who have taken away half of your face, confiscated one eye, and filled your mouth with 'concrete'?

I thought long and hard and decided that the best way was to buy them equipment which might give them a little less practice with the knife. The snag was that I had no money. If I'd had £100 in the bank I would willingly have given it. I really wanted to do something that would help other cancer sufferers to be treated more quickly and less painfully. I wanted to say thank you.

DOCATEF - the Detection of Cancer and Treatment Equipment Fund - was born just as I was recovering from my second lot of major surgery, in 1979.

I started to tell people about the idea, but I am sure they thought I was delirious; they said it was a good idea and they would help me, but the reaction seemed to be half-hearted and I am sure they were indulging me. I mentioned the idea to Mr. Knowles. At first he made nothing of it, but one day I went back to him and said: "Look, I was serious about the fund. Is there a piece of equipment I could buy that you will use for the benefit of other cancer patients?"

There was, he said, one item which would cost about £600. I said £600 was not much because I had thought of trying to raise £1,000, and he asked: "How much can you raise?"

Suddenly £1,000 did not seem much either, so I took a deep breath and said "£5,000" - but straightaway I wished I had kept my mouth shut because Mr. Knowles had obviously been hankering after a fibre-optic laryngoscope, and he said that would cost £5,000. It would enable him, he said, to do the same examination in six minutes in outpatients which was now causing patients to go into hospital, go to the theatre, and have to spend a week off work.

With this examination, the patient would not need an anaesthetic, and that clinched it. Knowing my own fear of my first anaesthetic, I said: "I will try to raise £5,000".

When I went out of the consulting room, I said to the girls on reception that I was going to try to raise the money, and asked them to help me. They agreed, but they wanted to know what the equipment was called. I couldn't remember, and a receptionist had to go back to Mr. Knowles to ask him to write it down.

Pat was waiting for me in the car and, immediately I got in, he asked: "What did Mr Knowles say?" I replied: "He wants a piece of equipment costing £5,000." Pat said: "I don't want to know what he wanted, I meant what did he say about you?"

"Oh, I forgot to ask him, but I must be all right because I am coming back next week." There and then Pat predicted: "You will never raise £5,000." £1,000 was a fortune. "You don't know enough people; you have bitten off more than you can chew." He went nattering on in the same vein when there was a knock on the window. I wound it down and there was a friend, Sheila Benton, from the hospital who looked aghast and said: "Oh, ducky, have you been in a car crash?"

I replied: "No, I have had cancer again, and now I am going to raise £5,000 for a piece of equipment, will you help me?" She said she would, and went on duty. On arriving home the telephone started ringing. I picked it up, and at the other end was the same friend I had been talking to a few minutes earlier. She said: "You will not believe it, Lyn, but I have a refund from my holiday payment – twenty pounds, will you have it for your first donation?" In triumph I turned to Pat and said: "There you are, I only need £4,980 now!"

This particular friend was so supportive, giving a pound here and a pound there, and suddenly I had thirty pounds, but she complained about having to write "Cancer Equipment Fund for Pilgrim Hospital" on cheques, so we had to come up with something shorter. That was when DOCATEF was born.

Although Pat was a 'Doubting Thomas' when I said I was going to raise £5,000, I think it was only because he was afraid that I had bitten off more than I could chew. From the word 'go', however, he supported me as he promised he would if he could stay in the background and if I did not press him to attend functions.

He was grateful to Mr. Knowles, and the staff at Pilgrim

Hospital, for saving my life, and one of the fund's first money-raising efforts was a sponsored walk from Eastville to Spilsby and back by Pat and our son Stephen which raised £150.

Typically they left early one morning so that no-one would see them and the only stop they made was to visit the toilet at a friend's house in Toynton.

Our daughter Kathy was staying with us at the time, and we followed Pat and Steven from the comfort of the car. This puzzled granddaughter Melanie, who wasn't quite five at the time. "Why don't you let my Grandy have a ride? Poor Grandy." she kept repeating all the time.

The fund was my way of saying "thank you" to Mr. Knowles and Pilgrim Hospital for the kind care and attention they had given me. The first time I was in hospital everything was new to me, and I was naive in the matter of health care. Five years on I was a qualified nurse, and nursing for secondary cancer was different. I was fully aware of the cost of medicines and appliances, and of how many personnel were involved, not just the nurses and surgeons, but anaesthetists, theatre staff, domestic staff, caterers, ward orderlies, X-ray and laboratory staff, occupational therapists and physiotherapists, and many others. So there I was, offering to raise money for equipment which might help Mr. Knowles in his fight against cancer.

Friends organised jumble sales and coffee mornings, and the money came in slowly . . . oh, so slowly, in dribs and drabs. Too slowly for my liking. The Fund wasn't really taking off. I was musing what to do about this one day when I was flicking through the pages of our weekly newspaper, the Lincolnshire Standard, and I spotted a sad story about a litte girl who had fallen out of a tree and had died of her injuries. The article was beautifully and sympathetically written, and I noted the name of the reporter: Pat Ashberry. I thought to myself: "I wonder if she would write something about my fund - something to capture the imagination of the public."

I did not feel sufficiently confident to talk on the telephone at that time, as I was recovering from surgery, so I wrote to Pat at the Boston office of the Lincolnshire Standard. I did not really expect her to reply but, after I had sent the letter I continued to think that I needed the publicity to set the fund on the way to its target, so I eventually plucked up the courage to call her on the telephone as a follow up to my letter.

From the first 'hello' we hit it off, and I arranged for Pat to come out to Eastville to see me, but constantly interrupted the interview by saying: "Don't put that in - I wouldn't like that in the paper - it wouldn't be a good idea to print that."

Eventually, but gently, she put me in my place by saying: "You can't expect to start a fund without saying something about the person who is starting it."

The article that Pat wrote from that first interview appeared in the Boston edition of the Lincolnshire Standard on October 19th 1979. It hit the right note, and afterwards the money came in like an avalanche. The 23,000 copies of the Standard that went out that week must have been read by some of the most generous people in the country - and Pat's article eased the money out of their pockets.

Since then Pat has become a good friend, and I always say that the success of DOCATEF is due to her and the Lincolnshire Standard. They have been so very good to me.

Two important telephone calls resulted from that first article. One was from Mrs. June Kemp, headmistress of the Conway School in Boston, and the other was from the Rev. Bill Hurdman, then vicar of Friskney. I had nursed Mrs. Kemp while she was in hospital, and she rang to see if I was the nurse she remembered. It was lovely to hear from her, and she promised her school would try to raise £100 for the fund. It was half-term and she said "Leave it with me - I'll be in touch." I heard no more until the week before Christmas but, when the telephone call came, Mrs. Kemp told me to sit down and wait for the good news.

"Blimey", I thought, "They have raised the £100. Oh, good."

Mrs. Kemp's voice came over loud and clear. "You must understand," she warned, "That we haven't collected all the money yet, but we had a count up this mornng and, so far, we have raised ... more than ... £1,000."

I was flabbergasted. How on earth had they managed to raise that much? Mrs. Kemp told me that the young children held sponsored walks round the playground, and the older ones did sponsored spelling and sums. Eventually the Conway children raised

£1,300 from that magnificent effort, and that set the trend for the extreme generosity of the Boston area people.

Then there was the call from the Rev. Bill Hurdman. We had met briefly when he called to see me in hospital. They nominated a charity of the month in their parish, and he had nominated DOCATEF for November. There was one snag, however, although the Rev. Bill saw no problem. He wanted me to talk about the fund at the coffee evening he was organising in my honour. At the very thought of talking in public, however small the gathering, my stomach churned and my legs turned to jelly despite my experience in selling Tupperware. My tonsils were well oiled, and my tongue quite capable of wagging with the best of them, but only in private and for a gossip among friends. I made all manner of excuses. He would listen to none, and it was against my better judgement that I made the short journey to Friskney. There was no going back. Surrounded by his family and friends, and parishioners, I told them about my fund. They listened quietly and politely - dare I say with real feeling and understanding - and you could have heard a tear drop. At the end of my talk I answered questions and, very much to my surprise, I was invited, there and then, to speak to a local Women's Institute.

Since then, simply because the Rev. Bill Hurdman refused to take 'no' for an answer, I have spoken up and down the county to lots of organisations, sometimes as many as five in a week. I have never made a charge. I have never wanted anything for myself, but I have gratefully accepted all the donations these people have made to DOCATEF. And they have, without fail, always been extremely generous.

In the early days of launching the fund, I always bought my own stationery and paid all the postage. I have tried to send a thank-you letter to everyone who has donated to, or helped, the fund, because I know how much I appreciate thank-you letters myself. I paid for my own petrol too, sometimes as much as eight pounds a week. But I was happy to give the money as well as my time because I was so glad of the help I had received, and so grateful for the chance to live a full life.

I kept the then administrator at Pilgrim Hospital, Mr. Martin Gibson, fully informed of my activities and invited him to listen to one of my talks. He accepted the invitation to a meeting of

Skegness Toc H which I was addressing and, after hearing what I had to say, one of his reactions was anger . . . anger that I was paying my own expenses while raising money for hospital equipment. He insisted that I claim for legitimate expenses in future.

In those early days I was grateful for the help of Mrs. Babs Hall, who was happy to act as treasurer and relieve me of the worry of keeping count of the ever increasing amount of money that was flooding in. She handled all the money, and liaised with the surgeons over the purchase of equipment, until she was unable to carry on the work.

As the fund-raising business boomed, and I was repeatedly in and out of hospital, I became concerned about the future of DOCATEF. I wanted it to be less dependent on me, and to survive if, and when, I could no longer carry on with the work. I talked over the problems with Mr Gibson's successor, Mr Bill Mortlock, and eventually we formed a committee to run the fund and succeeded in registering it as a charity.

Now I have a committee, invited because I like them all as friends, to supervise the running of DOCATEF. Mr. Mortlock's successor, Mr. Ken Dobson, sits in as adviser and link man with the needs of the hospital, and other members of the committee are:

Mrs. Noreen Evison, a nursing officer, who is well aquainted with the equipment needs of the hospital, and acts as committee secretary.

Mrs. Vicky Waltham, the treasurer, a friend who works in New Leake Post Office, so I thought she must be used to handling money!

Mr. Graham Rodwell, an accountant friend of Bill Mortlock, who acts as financial adviser, and who worked on our constitution to satisfy the Charity Comissioners.

Mr. James Knowles, the ear, nose, and throat surgeon who has done most of the demolishing and rebuilding that has kept me alive over the past twelve years or so.

Mrs. Audrey Hill, a good friend who has bullied me into continuing the fight whenever I have been feeling low, and who persuaded the Target newspaper to organise a fund to take Pat and me to Greece for a holiday with our daughter.

Mr. George Wheatman, Editor of the Boston and Sleaford

Target, who was editor of the Boston edition of the Lincolnshire Standard when they were so good in helping launch my appeal.

Mrs. Pat Ashberry, a journalist with the Lincolnshire Standard, whose articles have fired the sympathy and generous help of the local public.

Mrs. Sheila Robson, a much respected columnist with the Lincolnshire Free Press and Spalding Guardian whose articles have taken news of DOCATEF into the homes in South Lincolnshire.

Just a thought – if journalists are the despised, back-stabbing lot many people think they are, why is it I have three such 'gems' on my committee?

Mr. Richard Addlesee, a local undertaker. I didn't invite him because I was seeking a discount ... Richard's father was one of the first people to help DOCATEF and now his son has continued the good work. The fund has had thousands of pounds from collections and donations from families of many deceased. All the local funeral directors have been extremely helpful: Addlesee's were the first.

Mrs. Eirwen Thompson, my driver and almost constant companion on forays to boost the fund. She has shown great dedication to DOCATEF. I owe her so much. Her husband Arthur, although not a committee member, often acts as navigator and back seat driver on our forays.

Mrs. Jean Padley, latest addition to the committee, co-opted because she has always been so willing to help DOCATEF.

All members of the committee give their time willingly and, of course, quite freely.

DOCATEF – the initials and its achievements – crop up as frequently in this book as anything you read or hear of Lyn Ellis: the two are inseparable. Without the fund it is unlikely that you would ever have heard of Lyn Ellis.

Without Lyn Ellis having contracted cancer it is equally unlikely that DOCATEF would have been formed. Then maybe – although it is far from certain because someone else may have come along – Pilgrim Hospital might not yet have some of the equipment listed at the start of this book and which has been highlighted in newspsper reports over the years.

Having celebrated its seventh anniversary in October 1986, DOCATEF had now raised more than £216,000*, and more money is coming in almost daily.

I have one big wish and it is that, when I die, someone else will step forward and take my place. Someone to keep DOCATEF alive to help the fight against cancer in our loved ones.

---

* This figure is as at the time of going to press – see the back cover for the latest details that can be included.

11.

By Royal Invitation
(As told to the Swineshead Young Wives)

BECAUSE OF MY FUND WORK I received an invitation to Buckingham Palace - to a garden party. You may not believe it, but I do have a husband. He comes out only on special occasions - such as visits to The Palace.

Towards the end of March last year I was in bed when the telephone rang and the voice of a young lady asked: "Would you like to go to a garden party at Buckingham Palace?" It was nearly April 1st. Was it an April Fool's joke? Eventually convinced that it was not, I said, "Yes, please." "Have you a husband?" "Oh heck, yes!" "Have either of you a police record?" "Well, I once parked without lights." "We will be getting in touch with you."

Pat came into the bedroom, and I told him I had had a call from Buckingham Palace and, judging by the way the lady spoke, he would end up in the Tower. We didn't tell anyone - not even family.

A month passed and nothing happened and Pat said to me "You fibber." Then a letter arrived from the Chairman of the South Lincolnshire Health Authority confirming that we had been invited to the Palace, and giving us the choice of two dates. We decided on July 7th. Immediately we started saving our pennies because you can't go to Buckingham Palace in jumble sale rejects. I told a few friends about it, but it seemed impossible to tell anyone without seeming a bighead. I bought the material for a skirt and blouse for £10 and a friend made me a suit.

I was really bothered about the need for a comfortable pair of shoes and I decided that I should have to have an expensive pair so that meant economising elsewhere. Pat had to have his suit dry-cleaned and his shoes polished every day! But just so he had something new I bought him a new handkerchief.

I didn't have a hat to wear, but Pat Ashberry, the Lincolnshire Standard reporter who had become a good friend, offered me a straw boater.

We were planning to go down to London by bus but then came the offer of a chauffeur-driven car by local Ford dealers, Sandicliffe. That was marvellous. Sandicliffe had been 'primed' by friends at the Standard.

Then came the big morning, and I still had one worry. I can't open my mouth very wide and I am liable to make a mess while eating. I didn't want to wear a bib, or get messed up in a café. So, when we had a snack on the way down, I insisted we stop in a layby so that the wind blew the crumbs in the right direction!

Because we went by car we drove straight into Buckingham Palace. Talk about Lady Muck! I felt that way. Husband Pat felt a bit out of it because he did not have tails and a top hat. He needn't have worried. A man in front of us wearing a top hat and tails had the biggest of holes in his sock! I surmised that he could not afford to hire socks with his suit.

You had to look after your pass and make sure you had it available all the time. I have never seen such high walls. It was 92°F. and there were a lot of people on a lawn as big as Swineshead. I said to a man that I didn't feel very well. He stuttered and said that I couldn't sit down because everyone else would want to.

In front of the veranda was a half moon of chairs. I thought there was going to be a show. The brass band started to play the National Anthem. I saw the Queen on the veranda and the chairs began to fill up. Pat nudged me and said: "There's the Queen Mum." The crowd ran across the lawn to get a look at her, and they cheered. The Queen was followed by Prince Charles and Princess Diana. He had his arm round her lovingly.

My feet had swollen up. They were like Yorkshire puddings. I said to a man: "I am a cancer patient, can I sit down?" He gave me a chair and said: "Promise not to move, I shall be back in a quarter of an hour."

There was the Duke of Kent, and Princess Michael looked lovely. Princess Margaret was expected to come but didn't. We just sat there. A lot of people were fainting, but I have never seen such weak-looking stretchers as they had around that day, and I thought I was not going to try one of them.

The Queen came up so close. She turned and looked at me and on impulse I wanted to touch her to see if she was real. The man who had given us that chair knew that she would pass that way. It had been a lovely thought. Whether that was true or not I don't know, but a few minutes earlier it had seemed that everyone was going the wrong way.

There were 6,000 people there that afternoon. In the best tradition I stuck up my little finger and drank my orange squash. I dared not try the gateaux.

If you went by car you had a special card with your name and address and number of the car on it. 'Mr. and Mrs. P. N. Ellis'. Oh, I did feel posh when our names were called out, and I felt ever so grand for a few minutes as we walked down the red carpet. I bet the people who were waiting to see the Royal Family walk down that carpet were disappointed to see me! I can still hardly believe that we went to The Palace, but I would never have been able to go had not the community been so supportive and generous to the fund.

What surprised me about the Royal Family was how short they all were. The Queen was so petite. Diana had a lovely peaches-and-cream complexion and was looking up into Prince Charles' eyes. My husband seemed a foot taller than any of them. It was nice to see him without his braces and wellies!

It's an odd thing to say: "I'm lucky to have had cancer." Of course, I would much rather have been able to avoid the clutches of this dreadful, painful disease, but I have been lucky in the sense that it led me to start DOCATEF and that, in turn, has taken me to so many places, and enabled me to meet so many lovely people. It has been an exhilarating adventure. Maybe the story is told best through some of the articles that have appeared in the Lincoln-shire Standard over the years, starting with one, written by Pat Ashberry, which began it all in 1979.

It was headlined, in big type:

'SALUTE NURSE COURAGEOUS'
And it read:
Like nurses the world over, Lyn Ellis spends far more time worrying about other people than she does

about herself.

So it was completely in character when, a few weeks ago, she decided she would like to raise several thousand pounds for a piece of life-saving cancer-detecting equipment for Pilgrim Hospital, and wrote to the Standard asking for a bit of publicity.

Lyn herself, however, is not one for the limelight, and she told me so in no uncertain terms when I called to see her at her Eastville home. All she wanted was a bit of help to raise cash for the vital machine, and the less said about Lyn Ellis the better.

My difficulty is finding a way of telling Lyn's tale without using words like courage and pluck and spirit and bravery.

She made me promise not to make her sound like a heroine, but it's not easy, and I find I can't describe her as anything less than a very special sort of woman having heard how, after enduring a five hours and twenty minute major operation for cancer of the sinuses, which has left her facially deformed, all she can think of is getting back to her job of nursing old people, and raising money which will help other cancer victims.

"There's nothing special about me – I'm just a victim of circumstance," insists 42-year old Lyn who, before her illness, and operation in the summer, worked at the Gables, Spilsby, and hopes to be back there working on the wards on 1st November.

The equipment Lyn is raising money for is a fibre-optic laryngoscope, to be used by the Ear, Nose and Throat department, and is likely to cost about £5,000.

She said: "They were absolutely marvellous for the four weeks I spent in hospital at Pilgrim, and this is something I would like to do to help repay the debt."

Lyn and her husband Pat, who runs the Orchard House Kennels at Eastville, have three grown up children of their own, are grand-parents, and also have two younger foster children.

Lyn has nothing but praise for her husband and family, who have given her their utmost support since her operation.

"It was worse for my husband than it was for me," she said. "When you love someone you know how it must feel for them to see you in pain and not be able to do anything to help. He's been tremendous - coping with the house, the kennels, and the children, as well as fitting in hospital visits."

The couple's over-riding sense of humour is largely responsible for seeing them through this difficult period in their lives.

"We've got to laugh about it, and carry on for the sake of the family," she explained. After all, I might live until I am ninety, and if I spend the next forty years weeping on my bed, wouldn't I feel a right fool at the end of it?"

"You've got to live with it, or die from it, that's my philosophy. And it seems to be that I've been given another life for some reason, and I must do something with it, not sit around moping. I've had some terrific support and encouragement from the local commmunity who came in regularly when I was discharged from hospital first. That was really important to me - I needed a great deal of reassurance then," she said.

News of Lyn's fund has been circulated by word of mouth only so far, but already she has had a number of donations. A doctor and a chiropodist have promised to do a sponsored swim, and other people are going to organise a dance.

If you feel you would like to help the fund in any way - either by donations or organising a fund-raising event write to Mrs Lyn Ellis, Orchard House Kennels, Eastville, Boston, or ring New Leake 349.

That article, as I say, appeared in the Standard in October 1979, and I shall be eternally grateful to the newspaper and Pat Ashberry for the story that hit just the right note.

It quickly became obvious, too, that the Standard editor of that time - George Wheatman - was sympathetic to the cause, and encouraged Pat to keep my fund raising efforts in the public eye. George continued that support, and I received even wider coverage, when he moved over to the Linconshire Echo in October

1983, and then became editor of the new free distribution newspaper, the Boston and Sleaford Target, in March 1984.

This, and the welcome interviews of Sheila Robson, of the Lincolnshire Free Press and Spalding Guardian, enabled me to spread my fund-raising net far beyond the Standard territory.

But, in those early days, it was Pat and the Standard who truly launched DOCATEF and, along with it, yours truly.

Various other articles appeared, and the progress was meteoric! This was highlighted by another Standard article in April 1980 which read as follows:

Boston's Pilgrim Hospital last week received the second piece of specialist equipment for which Nurse Lyn Ellis, of Eastville, has been responsible. A third is on the way.

Nurse Ellis underwent a major operation last summer for cancer of the sinuses. After it, all she could think of was getting back to her job of nursing old people at The Gables Hospital at Spilsby - and raising money to help other cancer victims.

She set out to collect £5,000 for a fibroscopic laryngo-scope for the Ear, Nose and Throat department. That was delivered in February.

Then she set about raising another £5,000, this time for a flexible gastroscope which allows thorough examin-ation of the stomach without discomfort. This was handed over last week.

And now Nurse Ellis has raised £2,000 towards the £3,000 needed for a colposcope which is used to detect cancer of the cervix as well as purely routine inspections.

Her fund, to which she invites contributions, is called DOCATEF - Detection of Cancer and Treatment Equip-ment Fund. And she stresses that the equipment it has bought and is buying doesn't need the introduction of new specialist staff to operate it.

Contributing towards last week's equipment, apart from scores of individuals, were the Boston and District League of Hospital Friends (£521); Mrs Carol Burrill and friends, of Eastville (£337 from a dance); colleagues at The Gables (a dance raised £205); Mrs Hill and residents and friends of Crighton House for the elderly at Sibsey (£57); Stickney WI whist drive (£40); and a collection at E.Fogarty and Co. Ltd. (£100).

So now the fund was well and truly on its way, and I was meeting with wonderful people and experiencing their tremendous generosity.

The people in this part of the world may not be extroverts, they may live quietly in what, to many, may seem one of the country's backwaters, but the kindness, caring, and generosity of the Lincolnshire Yellow Belly cannot be surpassed. I am sure of that. I have witnessed it all at first hand, and all through this spontaneous giving I have reminded myself of the generally low wage levels in this part of the country. People have been willing to donate an amazingly high percentage of those earnings. That is something which makes me feel so very humble.

There was another progress report by Pat Ashberry in the Lincolnshire Standard in March 1981. By that time the fund stood at £29,000.

In this article Pat recalled:

Her courageous story moved many people, and help and cash came flooding in from schools, firms, children's and youth groups, women's organisations and individuals.

Elderly people sent a pound from their pension, schools organised sponsored events, colleagues and friends held coffee evenings and jumble sales.

So far the money has bought three costly pieces of equipment for different hospital departments, and several others are in the pipeline.

Said Lyn this week: "I think it is a wonderful tribute to the people in this community – it shows they are a caring community. Everybody cares about Pilgrim.

Until two or three months ago Lyn was working as a nurse at The Gables, at Spilsby, where she nursed old people, but she has recently been recuperating after another operation in London before Christmas. She has decided to retire in March.

But she still plans to carry on working for the fund, raising money for equipment to help others.

"I've been really touched by people's generosity. If it weren't for them the whole thing would have been nothing."

Personally I was even more touched by the paragraph that concluded that story. Unknown to me, Pat Ashberry had spoken to my husband Pat, and she added to the article the comment he made: "Without Lyn there would be no fund. I think she is rather special."

That brought tears to my eyes. It's rather special to hear kind words from someone you love. When those words are spoken in public they are even more special.

The year 1981 was a momentous one for me, and for DOCATEF. Together we seemed to be constantly in the news and it became a family joke if I was not mentioned in the Standard. "It's not worth buying this week," the kids would say, "You're not in it, Mum."

To my surprise I was elected Lincolnshire Standard Woman of the Year in 1981. I can only think it was because stories about me and my fund had filled so much of their space! I must admit, however, that the cutting marking the award has pride of place in my scrapbook. It is always nice to receive acknowledgement of anything you may have done. What's more, in my eyes, it was yet another tribute to the generosity of the Lincolnshire public.

It was the first of other such coveted awards received though none was ever sought.

There came an invitation to a Buckingham Palace Garden Party, a Civic Award from Boston Borough Council, and another tremendous gesture from the public when they rallied behind an appeal by the Boston Target and contributed £2,000 to send Pat and me to Greece on holiday.

The Civic Award is a special certificate given by the Boston Borough Council to local residents who they feel have contributed significantly to the community, and it is presented in front of the whole Council and invited guests. Boston Borough Council, I am told by people who know these things better than I do, have only sparingly used the honour of the Freedom of the Borough, and the Civic Award is a slightly scaled down version of this highest of all Borough honours.

To receive that Civic Award from the hands of the Mayor of that time, Councillor Cyril Fovargue, was indeed an honour, and one of the moments in my life that I shall always remember, only to be surpassed by the ultimate honour, the Freedom of the Borough of Boston. More about that later, however.

Back to that first award - the Lincolnshire Standard Woman of the Year. I'll let the Standard tell the story themselves, again through the words of Pat Ashberry:

The headlines screamed: **'Salute our Woman of the Year'** and: **'Courageous Lyn One in a Million'.** The report underneath read:

The first thing Lyn Ellis said when she heard she'd won the Woman of the Year contest - once she'd got her breath back - was: "I never thought I'd win - the others are much more deserving than I am." Our readers and judges didn't think so - their votes overwhelmingly gave Lyn the title. But, having said that, all our nominees were marvellous women, and if it had been possible I would have given them all the title.

We promised to help the charity of the winner's choice, and are therefore making an appeal for Lyn on behalf of DOCATEF, the fund she started 18 months ago and has worked for unceasingly since, despite at the outset having only just recovered from a major operation, and in addition to working at The Gables Hospital and looking after her home and children too.

The fund raises money for cancer detecting equipment for Pilgrim Hospital - equipment which the hospital would have to do without otherwise, simply because it has not got enough cash to buy it.

Early detection of cancer is vital - it means the difference between saving a life and losing it.

Already Lyn's fund has raised money for several instruments which are in use at Pilgrim Hospital every day in different clinics.

Unlike some large charities, DOCATEF gives every penny it raises towards buying equipment. Lyn buys her own stationery, writes her own thank you letters, buys her own postage stamps, her friends use their own petrol ferrying her to and from meetings, so every penny you give helps someone.

I said when I first wrote about Lyn that it was difficult to tell her story without the use of words like courage and pluck, and spirit and bravery.

I have got to know her a lot better over the months since, and my great respect and admiration for her grows each time I talk to her.

In the words of her husband Pat, she's very special. And she deserves all our support.

On the same page in the same issue Pat Ashberry also wrote:

Former nurse Lyn Ellis would be the first to admit that it's not often she's lost for words. But a telephone call from this office recently left her speechless.

The call was to pass on the news to Lyn that readers and judges - the Mayor and Mayoress of Boston, the editor George Wheatman, and myself - had resoundingly voted her as their Woman of the Year.

Said Lyn at her home at The Kennels, Station Road, Eastville, after she had time to take it in: "It's a great honour - but I still can't believe it.

All I can say is what I have said all along - it's the marvellous generosity of the people who've helped and donated who have made the fund such a success."

The fund she was talking about is, of course, DOCATEF (Detection of Cancer and Treatment Equipment Fund) which she began 18 months ago in October 1979, and which has now topped a staggering £30,000.

"People have been just marvellous. I can't thank everyone enough," she said. "The fund wouldn't have come to anything if it wasn't for people's generosity."

There are plenty of people who know that is not entirely true, of course - that it's Lyn's courage, humour, enthusiasm and gentle concern for others that really got the fund off the ground.

It was in the late summer of 1979, after Lyn's life

had been saved by a major five-hour operation at Pilgrim Hospital, for cancer of the sinuses, that she felt she would like to repay her debt to the hospital in some way.

That way, she eventually decided, was to open a fund to raise money for equipment with which to detect and treat cancer, although many of the instruments the fund has bought are also for the detection of other ailments.

She made her first public appeal through the columns of The Standard, and the response was immediate and heart-warming - and took Lyn's breath away.

Money and offers of help flooded in from schools, firms, children's groups, women's organisations, churches, and individuals.

Elderly people sent a pound from their pensions, schools organised sponsored events, people Lyn had never met organised slim-ins and coffee mornings and jumble sales, pubs made collections and held marathons.

The fund caught everyone's imagination, and soon Lyn found herself spending all her precious spare time when she wasn't nursing old people at The Gables, at Spilsby, writing thank you letters for donations, or speaking to different groups all over this part of the county about her illness, her job, her family - and her fund.

In the months since, Lyn has had to retire from nursing last month, which means she can now spend more time working for the fund.

"I like to write a personal hand-written letter of thanks to every person who makes a donation," she said. "People have said I ought to duplicate them, but I think a personal letter means much more to people.

It takes me hours - I often get up at 6.00 a.m. or stay up late to get them written.

We get a lot of help now from people who have lost relatives and send a donations to us instead of having flowers. I'm very grateful to those people - I think it's a lovely gesture for them to make at such a sad time, and I try to write a few words of comfort and thanks to them for helping me fight cancer in this way." said Lyn.

She regularly spends two or three evenings a week giving talks to clubs and organisations, and because she can no longer drive, she is driven by friends who have organised a rota.

Many groups, Lyn feels, are a little apprehensive about her talk before they hear what she has to say. They think that because she is a nurse she may frighten them with too much detail about her illness.

Their fears are entirely unfounded, of course, and Lyn's talk usually turns into one big laugh for the audience as her marvellous sense of humour begins to take over.

Children have responded particularly well to Lyn's appeal and she loves visiting schools and talking to the young pupils.

It took Lyn a while initially to accept that publicity for her beloved DOCATEF automatically meant publicity, too, for Lyn Ellis.

Now she's used to being photographed, and Lyn in her piratical eye-patch - worn because of bad double vision in one eye caused by the operation - is a familiar face in the pages of the Standard.

She told me, with a chuckle, that she was thinking of getting a parrot for her shoulder.

It's a remark that's typical of her sort of humour and courage that, together with the supportive help of her family and the magnificent response of a caring community, has brought Lyn Ellis through the past difficult months, and ensured vital and practical help for other cancer victims like her.

Yes, I was thrilled by that Lincolnshire Standard award and it was, perhaps, the first time that I had realised the rapport that had developed between the public and myself. People had been so wonderful, and had responded to my appeal in a manner I had not thought possible.

Of course we all love to be thanked, to receive a little acknowledgement for what we have done, however small. I am no exception, and I received the Woman of the Year award with a great deal of pleasure.

It was another boost in my fight against cancer. Inside a year my spirits were sent soaring again, this time by Boston Borough Council. They gave me their Civic Award, something they had introduced to reward people who have given special service to the community.

By this time the fund had reached about £45,000 so it was really all those people who had raised that money who were responsible for my honour. They were sharing it with me. It was nice though, to have the Council's gratitude and to enjoy the special night when, in a packed council chamber, I received the certificate from the Mayor, Councillor Cyril Fovargue.

I don't have to have a swig of whisky, or a shot of anything, to put me on a 'high'. All I need is people; people to talk to, to joke with, people to share my experiences with. On that particular night, surrounded by friends and the Borough's civic leaders, I was drunk with delight, and still tingle at the thought of councillors noting what DOCATEF had done in that way.

12.

MORE FUNDS, MORE EQUIPMENT - AND MORE OPERATIONS

IN MARCH 1982, with the fund standing at £46,000, I set my sights on raising another £25,000 for a special piece of equipment - the most costly sought so far - a laser capable of treating many kinds of cancer. Again people responded magnificently and, within a year, we had been able to purchase the life-saving laser. Only it was not £25,000 - it was £33,000.

Let me hand you over to the Lincolnshire Standard once again. They told the story at the time when the laser was officially handed over to Pilgrim Hospital:

DOCATEF, the fund that's become a household name in the Boston area in recent years, had its biggest triumph with the handover to Pilgrim Hospital of a £30,000 life-saving laser.

The laser, bought with cash raised by many local organisations and from hundreds of individual donations large and small, will save countless patients from the surgeon's knife, and will make Pilgrim Hospital the envy of hospitals up and down the country.

The £30,000 laser can be used by all the surgeons of Pilgrim for cancer and many other benign operations and, in the hands of the right surgeons, could have been used to operate on the young boy in the news recently when his parents raised many thousands of pounds to send him to America for a laser operation on a spinal tumour.

Since then it has become known that other hospitals in the country have the same laser facilities, and now Pilgrim is one of those elite few.

The equipmemt was handed over by Lyn Ellis

on behalf of DOCATEF to the hospital at a special ceremony attended by the deputy Mayor and Mayoress, Councillor and Mrs. Keith Lancaster, hospital staff, and friends of DOCATEF.

Consultant E.N.T. surgeon Mr. Graham Westmore told the gathering that sometimes pieces of equipment given to hospitals were not used.

"But," he said: "Rest assured, the laser has been around for 20 years and is well established. This equipment which you have laboured so spendidly to provide, is going to be used in a big way.

A machine like this is only as good as the people who use it, and we are going to do our very best to justify this spendid gift."

The fund, begun by Lyn Ellis nearly three and a half years ago as a thank you to staff at Pilgrim for saving her life with a major operation for cancer of the sinuses, has now raised an incredible £72,000.

About £57,500 has been spent, and another £14,500 is in hand ready for the next piece of equipment – this time a haemotology freezer unit for use in connection with bone marrow transplants.

Lyn's fund began to appeal for money for equipment for the treatment of cancer and other complaints in October 1979.

Within four months her first piece of equipment – a laryngoscope costing about £5,000 – was delivered and handed over to Mr. J. E. A. Knowles, the consultant E.N.T. surgeon who performed Lyn's own operation.

Next came a gastroscope and later a fibre-optic gastroscope and light source for Dr. M. J. Fairman's department, then a light source and several pieces of equipment for the E.N.T. Department, a bronchoscope for Dr. Cyril Nyman, diathermy apparatus and an electro-surgical generator for Mr. P. C. Watson and, finally, the £33,000 laser for the use of all the surgeons.

The laser will eliminate the surgeon's knife in many cases, and will ease Pilgrim Hospital's waiting list substantially as patients are often discharged after two days following laser surgery, compared with anything up to a fortnight's stay for a conventional operation.

I was pleased with that article in the Standard because it was the first time the equipment bought by DOCATEF had been listed so that members of the public, who had donated so generously, could see for themselves just how their money had been spent.

Little did I realise that, within nine months of that presentation night, the laser would become a lifeline for me.

Since I am relying so heavily on the Lincolnshire Standard for telling this part of the story, I will hand you over to Pat Ashberry again. A week before Christmas 1983 she told her readers:

> The £30,000 laser bought by Lyn Ellis's DOCATEF appeal is to be used this week on Lyn herself in a life-saving cancer operation.
> Courageous Lyn, the 46-year-old former nurse who began raising money for equipment for Pilgrim Hospital four years ago after conventional surgery for cancer of the sinuses, was just getting over another operation carried out in London in the autumn when she was told a fortnight ago that the original disease had recurred. She was due to have intricate laser surgery on her cheek.
> Said Lyn before being taken to the theatre at Pilgrim: "When DOCATEF handed over the laser in February, I never dreamed it would ever be used on me. It's ironical. I certainly never planned it this way. If it wasn't for DOCATEF and people's generosity, Pilgrim wouldn't have the laser, and I would have to have more conventional surgery which takes much longer to get over.
> Lyn's first operation which affected the sight in her right eye and resulted in her wearing the distinctive black patch she's now so well known for, was in July 1979. She spent several weeks in Pilgrim afterwards, and it was when she got home and began to recover from major surgery that she decided to try to raise some money for a piece of equipment for the E.N.T. department as a way of saying thank you to surgeons, doctors, and nurses for saving her life.
> Her first goal was £5,000, a sum which Lyn thought at the time was, perhaps, a little ambitious. But her

story touched the hearts of thousands and the money flooded in.

To date DOCATEF has raised about £82,000 and various hospital departments are using the equipment to save lives every day.

The laser was the most expensive item purchased by the fund. It cost in the region of £30,000 and DOCATEF also paid for the first year's running costs, and the first five years' maintenance for it, a total altogether of £33,000.

The laser works by using a concentrated beam of light which turns to heat and acts in the place of a surgeon's knife.

But the beauty of it is that as it burns it seals off all the tiny blood vessels, preventing bleeding, and, as a result, follow up nursing care is reduced and the patient recovers much more quickly.

"I was in hospital for weeks after my first operation, but this time I should be home in a matter of days," explained Lyn.

And she added: "You mustn't give people the idea I'm ill. I'm not ill. I've just got some malignant cells that they're going to get rid of. Of course it was a blow when I heard the cancer had come back again, but it's just a hiccup. I shall soon be fighting fit again.

I've been unlucky getting it, but I've been lucky being cared for at Pilgrim. They really do care, and I couldn't be in better hands.

Early in 1984 DOCATEF was registered as a charity, and the task of running it and supervising the spending of money raised was shared by a committee of which I was elected Chairman (or should it be Chairperson?). I hope that this reorganisation will ensure the continuation of the fund for many years to come.

There continued to be regular reports in the local papers about the fund and the marvellous efforts people were making to raise money, but the next major 'milestone' was reported by the Standard in June 1984 under the headline:

Laser Op For Fundraiser

That report told the Boston public:

Champion fund-raiser Lyn Ellis is in hospital in Southampton where she was to undergo two laser operations
for cancer this week.

Lyn, a former nurse, of Station Road, Eastville,
was referred by Pilgrim Hospital to Southampton so
that she could be treated by the surgeon who pioneered
laser surgery.

She has had a number of operations in Pilgrim, as
well as major surgery last autumn at King's College
Hospital, London.

The laser to be used on Lyn works in conjunction
with a special technique involving the injection of a
dye to show up any malignant tumours which can then
be accurately removed by laser.

The disadvantage is that it causes the skin to become
sensitive to light, and after the operation Lyn has been
told she must be totally covered for a month.

But, typically, Lyn's not letting it worry her and
is determined to get back into the swing of her fund
raising activities for DOCATEF as soon as she can,
even if it means getting out and about incognito in
head-to-toe drapes!

"I shall have to make sure I wear my eye patch so
that people know who I am." Lyn joked, the day before
her hospital admission.

At that stage the fund stood at £105,000.

Two months later, when the Standard informed their readers
of my progress after the Southampton operation, that figure had
increased to £110,000.

On that occasion the report read as follows:

Boston's favourite fund raiser Lyn Ellis is running true
to form. After the latest in a series of operations
for cancer, brave Lyn is bouncing back once more with
only the courage and resilience that's made her a legend
in her own lifetime in the town and surrounding districts.

Lyn, whose DOCATEF appeal has now reached

118

£110,000 in the little less than five years since she began it, had her latest operation done with special laser equipment at a Southampton hospital in July, and says there have been some dark times since then.

But now she's on the mend, and can't stop telling everyone how well she feels.

"I've had some marvellous news - the surgeon says he's 99 per cent sure I'm clear of cancer. Cure is a word they don't use, and it's a word I'm a bit wary of. But that operation and that lovely piece of news have made such a difference to me. I feel as though I'm starting to live again."

Lyn made it clear, however, that though she feels fine, and better than she's felt for years, she still has her limitations, and is prepared to accept them.

"You can't be ill for eleven years and suddenly go back to your old lifestyle. My trouble is that I'm out of condition, and I'm trying to put that right."

Something not many people know about Lyn is that as a teenager she was an accomplished long-distance swimmer. She used to swim Morecambe Bay - she lived in the Bradford area - and round the castle foot at Scarborough. And she planned to swim the channel, but fell in love, married, and got pregnant instead.

Now she feels she's beaten her illness she's taken up swimming again, and was recently delighted when she managed to swim six lengths of Boston pool.

She's bought herself an exercise bicycle, too, and regularly takes little jaunts twice a day, in the privacy of her own bedroom (though her husband Pat - a bit of a card - invariably asks if she wants some sandwiches packing!)

And, best of all, Lyn has lost about four and a half stones as the result of a strict diet over the past twelve or thirteen months, and she is thrilled with her new slimmer figure.

The improvement in her health and general condition means Lyn is now back working for DOCATEF once more, visiting clubs and organisations to talk about the fund and the good it's doing at Pilgrim Hospital.

raising money for equipment that's saving lives there every day.

"I'm so glad to be back working for the fund again," says Lyn, "though I'm going to be careful not to overdo it. I have to accept that I have my limitations still. I'm fine swimming or on the bike, but I'm still not very good on my feet - I think it's because I haven't done much walking since I first became ill."

It is ten and a half years since she was first told she had cancer of the sinuses and, after treatment, she was all right for five years before illness struck again, and she's had numerous operations since, all but three at Pilgrim Hospital.

Lyn has very special feelings for Pilgrim - it was their love and care that prompted her to set up DOCATEF in October 1979 after her first major operation a few months earlier, and she only had her recent operation at Southampton because the equipment was not available here.

"If I hadn't been kept in such good condition by Pilgrim Hospital these past eleven years, I wouldn't have been alive to benefit from the special laser at Southampton. Pilgrim have kept me going all that time, and I can't thank them enough."

There have been some difficult times for her over the past five years, times when she was ill, depressed and in pain, her body battered, her spirit bruised. But she never let it show. There was always a smile, a bit of banter, or a joke.

"There have been some bad times," Lyn admits. "But when you are feeling better you forget about them. It's like having a baby - afterwards you forget the pain and remember only the joy. I've tried not to make a fuss about my illness, if you sat and moaned all the time, no one would want to know. I just count my blessings . . .

I'm beginning to feel fit now, though you mustn't give people the idea that I'm in peak condition - that's a long way off yet. But I do feel better than I have

120

for ages - you never know, I could be a Super-Gran one day!"

This feeling of getting better was tremendous. I was beginning to enjoy life again, but it was not all sunshine. There were good days and bad days.

In 1985 - in the middle of the year, although we had been building up to it over a number of weeks - there was another boost in the long, long fight against this dreaded disease. I was given a new face, and I felt I had to tell the Standard about it because, had the public not been warned, they would not have been able to recognise me without my pirate's patch!

This is how the Standard broke the news, with another Pat Ashberry story:

Boston's courageous cancer victim and champion fund raiser Lyn Ellis, has just come through one of the most anxious and exciting weeks of her life.

After lots of fittings, and a few doubts, Lyn is now facing up to the world with what she calls her 'new face'.

Forty-eight-year-old Lyn's brand new look has been brought about with the aid of something known in medical terms as a prosthesis, coupled with the skills of a specialist technician whose job is to rebuild faces shattered by accident, surgery or burns.

Lyn went home last week after a final fitting wearing new glasses which are specially designed to incorporate an artificial eye and cheek, necessitated by recent facial operations.

Lyn decided to talk about her new face, and be photographed because she felt it might help other people like her who have to have something similar after an accident or surgery, and are worried about it.

"It's something people are very nervous and embarrassed about, so perhaps talking like this might help. And anyway," she added with a smile, "I want people to recognise me still. I look rather different without my black patch."

Lyn had attended Pilgrim's outpatients' department

a number of times for the prosthesis to be designed and fitted.

It's literally a work of art. Lyn's own hair has been used to make an eyebrow and eyelashes, and the technician spent ages trying to find the exact colour to match Lyn's good eye - and found he had problems because her eye-colour subtly changes depending on what colour she happens to be wearing!

When he couldn't find an exact match, he painstakingly painted in flecks of colour until he got it just right, and during another of Lyn's visits he carefully painted matching freckles on the artificial cheek.

Lyn said she warned him she might not 'take to it' despite all his work, but now she has got it she's very pleased, though her first public appearance was quite an ordeal.

Said Lyn "It took more courage than I've ever needed before to walk out of that clinic wearing it. But the girls in reception, who knew all about it, were marvellous, and no one else seemed to take any notice. I really did feel thoroughly unsure of myself and completely lacking in confidence for those first few minutes, but it hasn't taken much getting used to."

The prosthesis will have to be replaced quite soon, however, as Lyn was due to go into Pilgrim again unexpectedly for more surgery, and it is expected that a new one will have to be made to fit her afterwards.

In the meantime, however, Lyn's enjoying putting her new face forward, and it has turned out to have one unexpected advantage - she'll be able to wink properly now that she's got two eyes.

"My grandson will be thrilled. He's always winking at me, and now I can wink back." Lyn says.

July 31st is my sister Beryl's birthday. It was also the day of my first post operation clinical appointment in Southampton during the summer of 1984.

That long, long trip to Southampton. I hadn't prepared well for it. I'd had a bad night and had only just found sleep when I was aroused by the early morning call. I was more tired than when

I had gone to bed the previous night, but it was useless trying for a few more minutes so I got out of bed and spent ten minutes on my exercise bike in an attempt to wake myself up. I pedalled away furiously and, as the wheel spun, it reminded me of Hammy, the children's pet hamster, long since dead, treading away at his wheel.

We set off for Southampton at 6.00 a.m., Bill, my ever generous and cheerful chauffeur, the ladies, and I. Remember? You were introduced to all three earlier. Well into the journey the sun burst through and I was glad Pat had reminded me to bring a sheet to wrap round my shoulders and hands to prevent my skin being exposed to the sunlight.

We arrived at Southampton at 11.30 a.m. and, by now, the sun was shining brightly. I made my way to the Ear, Nose, and Throat Clinic and, after queueing, gave my name, only to be asked: "Are you sure you have an appointment? I haven't got you on my list."

Blimey, I thought, not expected after a five and a half hour journey!

I explained that I had telephoned Mr. Carruth's secretary and she had told me to go that day. More searching of lists to no avail before I persuaded the receptionist to track down Mr. Carruth.

She did, and I was expected. Whew! What a relief.

I was able to tell Mr. Carruth that I was feeling quite well but that my worst problem was that my obturator wouldn't fit, and food fell out of my nose, and that I hadn't been able to speak. The problem had been solved temporarily. I was asked to remove the plate and 'open wide' which, in my case, was the width of one finger but there was just enough room for the examination. Mr. Carruth took his time and the long silence worried me. Then he said: "It looks good. On first examination it looks a bit suspicious but it is just skin tissue and everything looks fine to me.

I don't plan to see you any more. In fact you probably won't have any recurrence for a decade and even that would only mean you coming back for further laser surgery. It's still under control."

Mr. Carruth said the surgery had exceeded his hopes. The tumour had been removed simply when, in fact, he had expected difficulties. He shook my hand and said: "I hope everything goes well. You deserve it. You're a survivor."

I often reflect on how different my days are now compared with those early in my marriage to Pat. The only thing that hasn't changed is that the day begins, and ends, with a kiss from him.

At the start of our marriage Pat wanted a wife who looked after him; now he has a wife who needs, it seems, constantly looking after - and he does it so well.

So what is a typical day as I enter my fiftieth year?

It starts between 7.30 and 8.00 a.m. when I become aware that Pat is getting up. I feel cold and my face is hurting. Pat kisses me good morning. That never fails to give me a little thrill and I snuggle down again, pull the bedclothes tightly round me and doze off again.

Half an hour later Pat brings me a mug of hot mint tea and my medication to bring me more alive: one selenium tablet; two 50mg Voltarol tablets; one Diconal tablet; and two teaspoonsful of Erythromycin. The Selenium tablet I buy from the health food shop. It has been proved that it reduces tumours in animals. I have been taking it only a short time. I feel I have nothing to lose by taking it and I did consult my surgeon before deciding to add it to my morning dose of tablets. It also contains vitamins A and E.

The Voltarol is for my arthritis. I have 100 mg in the morning and again last thing at night. The Diconal is a strong pain-killer. I take one at four-hourly intervals. The Erythromycin is for an infection in my face.

I drink the tea hot. On very cold mornings, Pat brings up a hot water bottle. I feel the cold very quickly and the cold brings on the pain. I don't get up early unless I have any pressing engagements, so I snuggle down again until the post arrives at about 10.30 a.m. It is a rare day if I receive no letters. I love opening them.

Most of the mail is about DOCATEF matters, either donations or invitations to speak to local organisations about the fund. I can't read these days without the help of glasses, and Pat partly opens the curtains to throw in more light. By this time Pat will have lit 'Efel' - the affectionate name we gave long ago to our solid fuel boiler which provides the heating, and means for cooking.

We can't afford to keep her going night and day, so Pat has the daily chore of coaxing her back into action.

She responds quickly, however, and heats ten radiators so the bedroom is soon warm. I dress in the bathroom, after I have washed and cleaned my mouth. Now . . . my mouth is not quite normal. That is the one thing that has changed dramatically since we were married. In fact there is much less of my face generally.

I have very little palate and very little cheek on the right side. I have lost my right eye and eyelids. I syringe through the hole in my face, then clean the area with gauze swabs. I have lost the ability to blow my nose so this is an area that needs attention.

I can open my mouth wide enough to get one finger in. The surgeons and hospital technicians have fitted me with an obturator to replace my palate, cheek, and teeth. Without it I cannot speak, eat, or drink.

I clean this as part of the early morning ritual, and I clean my own remaining teeth. The obturator is held in place by normal suction and wires which are fixed, like an anchor, round one of my teeth.

I can use only a child's small toothbrush. I can see what I am doing by looking into the mirror just above the bathroom washbasin. I have to put my bottom partial denture in first, then the obturator. It's a work of art and fits like the last piece of a jigsaw puzzle.

Breakfast is of muesli and hot water - no milk - and a cup of mint tea. Pat fetches fresh mint in from the garden when it is available, and I buy mint tea bags to take with me wherever I go.

I have a home help who does the major house cleaning jobs twice a week, but I tidy up and do the washing up.

I try to write at least three letters each day. My friends are very understanding and know I don't mean to neglect replying to their letters. I always give priority to replying to DOCATEF correspondence, especially where donations have been made in lieu of flowers at funerals. I hope my letters bring a little comfort to the bereaved.

I drive down to the village alone to do my little bit of shopping.

125

I don't like driving in the town unless Pat or Danny accompanies me, and I can't see well enough to drive at night.

During the daytime at home I don't wear my famous black patch or glasses, which have been specially made for me and have an eye fixed on them. But if someone knocks at the door I panic until I have got one or the other on because I wouldn't want to upset anyone who might be squeamish, and I know I am not a pretty sight without them.

After writing my letters, I do the packed lunches for Stephen and Danny, if they are at home at the time, and then start to prepare the evening meal. I hate preparing vegetables so if anyone is at home and offers to help I am only too willing to accept.

Pat likes a pudding every day, and we all sit down together for our evening meal.

While waiting to start cooking dinner, I sit and read my Bible. I buy two books, *Every Day With Jesus* and *Daily Bread*, which guide me so that I don't just read at random.

I pray a lot. Not just night or in the morning, but also during moments of quietness during the day.

After the main meal of the day, we all share the washing up although sometimes, if I am going out on a speaking engagement, I am 'excused'.

I love going out to speak. I enjoy the company. My friend Eirwen Thompson, who has been a tremendous help and support, calls to drive me anywhere in the county to tell people about DOCATEF.

It is often 11.00 p.m. or later when we arrive home. Pat has 'Efel' burning nice and warm and the cylinder is bubbling with hot water. After a drink of cherry brandy and lemonade, I have to go through the ritual of cleaning my mouth again.

My hair is long so I have to put it up in a shower cap. Pat says I would scare anyone if they saw me like that. We laugh – if we didn't we'd probably both cry.

I have my bath and fold my clothes in the airing cupboard so that they will be warm in the morning. Pat always gets into bed first and lies on my side so that I get into a warm bed.

We kiss goodnight – and then I pray . . . silently.

13.

ON THE AIR

THE DAY BEFORE I received the Freedom of the Borough of Boston - and what an unbelievable, happy day that was - I featured in a Radio Lincolnshire broadcast 'In conversation with Trevor Hancock'.

As usual, it seems, I had a lot to say: too much, in fact, for the time allotted to the programme and my choice of music.

So, just to make sure that you do not escape from the pearls of wisdom which Methodist minister, the Reverend Trevor Hancock, 'prised' out of me, I thought it would be a good idea to reproduce - thanks to Trevor - the complete text of that interview.

Seriously . . . this is not an ego trip. It's just that I thought it might help to explain further, and perhaps a little more fully, my outlook on life with cancer. On reflection, in answer to the sensitive questioning by Trevor, I seem to have said some things I haven't said before. Or at least said them differently!

I started by explaining the origins of DOCATEF . . .

DOCATEF gets its name - in capital letters - from the Detection of Cancer and Treatment Equipment Fund. We had to use the abbreviation because there just isn't room on the cheques to write everything that you want, and so that's how DOCATEF got its name.

It was started as a thank you to Pilgrim Hospital and the surgeon who treated me for cancer. At that time I had already been a cancer patient for several years and I had had a remission for five years, and then it had come back.

I had had major surgery and, I think, being a nurse had made me more aware of the expense, and the number of people involved, in getting me well.

Had I been someone who was well off I would have given a donation to Pilgrim and thought I had done my bit but, as most people know, I am not very well off financially. It worried me because I couldn't give anything to the hospital but, after a great deal of thought, it occured to me that I could, perhaps, start a fund to buy a piece of equipment for Pilgrim Hospital which would benefit other cancer patients, and it was something I *could* do. I couldn't *give* but I could *do.*

I think, at first, everybody thought I was delirious and were being kind to me, and said they would help. After I had been discharged from hospital I did start a fund and people did support me.

The first piece of equipment was going to cost £5,000 and, within four months, the money was raised.

It was unbelievable and we discovered to our joy that, because the money came from the public [and was for medical equipment for treatment], the equipment was exempt from VAT. In actual fact, the £5,000 piece of equipment cost only £3,851 and there was money left over.

At this time I was having problems and was being treated by another doctor at the hospital who badly wanted a gastroscope . . ."

I think I must have paused for breath there, or perhaps Trevor was pleased I mentioned the word gastroscope, because that gave him a chance to remind listeners that he was still around. He was able to get in two words: "What's that?" and I was off again.

"A gastroscope detects cancer in the oesophagus, the stomach, and the duodenum, but it can also be used for innocent things like ulcers and warts, and so on.

DOCATEF never put their name on equipment we buy because you could get somebody going in for something quite innocent, see the name DOCATEF, and have unneccessary worries.

Trevor: "You started off wishing you could give a fiver and ended up thinking it wasn't enough, and it's gone on and on. How much does it stand at now - The Fund?"

"It's between £174,000 and £175,000. It's a terrific amount but I haven't raised this money myself. The money has come from the kind, generous, and caring people in the catchment area for Pilgrim Hospital which is Boston and then right out into the country. There's Skegness, Sleaford, Spalding, parts of Grantham, and all the villages in between, and everybody's been generous.

If, like me, they haven't been able to give anything, they have done something and raised money. People are wonderful. So please don't say I have raised it. It's the people in the community."

Trevor: "From all kinds of sources? From pubs and weddings and raffles?"

"You name it, it's been done. I remember when we first started the fund, the headmistress of Conway School in Boston rang me up and offered to do something and, in fact, they raised £1,300. When I asked how, she said the four-year-olds had done a sponsored walk in the playground, and the older children had done sponsored spells. So the very young have done their bit.

And also you could go right up the scale to the pensioners, and they are very, very generous. They have been very supportive."

Trevor: "You have said that it was raised by other people and not by you, but at the back of it is Lyn Ellis and, I think, without Lyn Ellis there would be no DOCATEF, so what I want to know, Lyn, is what makes you tick, because you are not cured, that's quite definite. Your cancer has little rests, and then it seems to spurt off again. "It likes me! I think that's the only way I can put it. I've had the best treatment. I have been treated many times in Pilgrim Hospital. I have been to Southampton and I have been to London, and always Pilgrim Hospital comes out on top.

We are so lucky. People don't realise how lucky we are to have such a modern hospital with the facilities they have got here."

Trevor: "Perhaps you two click - Lyn Ellis and Pilgrim Hospital, but your kind of cancer, Lyn, it's something that's fairly obvious isn't it, one has to say this."

"Well . . . the number of times I wished I had it where most ladies have it - in the breast, where you could wear a padded bra and no-one would know. But mine is obvious; if I didn't wear my patch people would be upset to see me."

Trevor: "Below the eyepatch is, in fact, a cavity where your right eye used to be. And other parts of your face and mouth have been removed?"

"Yes, I am bionic. I lost most of my palate, my cheek, my jaw, my teeth. I have even lost my eyelids and part of my face. I have what they call a prosthesis and obturator in my mouth. Without it I couldn't eat or speak or drink, and this wonderful piece of plastic - really that's what it is - enables me to speak and lead a normal life.

I can't open my mouth wide, can't eat a cream biscuit because the two biscuits together are too thick. I can just get a digestive biscuit in my mouth. That is as wide as my mouth will open."

Trevor: "The other thing is, Lyn, that you can't taste or smell."

"I can't taste or smell but I enjoy my food because each different food has a different texture. For example, nuts taste different to cornflakes, or whatever, so I do enjoy my food and I remember the taste and the smell - and I still have a weight problem."

Trevor: "You are on a diet. In fact, you can't taste or smell, so food doesn't have the same kind of attraction for you. Once you weighed . . . what was it? . . . nineteen stones? You have come down considerably since then."

"I came down because I knew I was going to have surgery and I knew I was silly anyway getting up to that weight but, when I first started with cancer twelve years ago, I felt ill and tired, and the only satisfaction I got out of life at that time was eating. When I knew I had cancer I knew I couldn't go through life being a cancer patient and weighing nineteen stones. I did lose weight then."

Trevor: "At the moment you are on a special diet

which is a bit bland anyway, because it seems, from what you have described to me, it has taken a lot of joy out of eating."

"Well, I read about it. It's the Bristol Cancer Diet, and it's vegetarian, almost vegan. For the first three months you are not allowed meat, or any dairy produce, cheese, butter, or eggs. It's easier to tell you what I can eat rather than what I can't."

Trevor: "You can't eat any kind of steak, or chops, or anything like that."

"No. In any case I have difficulty in chewing meat.

Trevor: "Because you can't open your mouth?"

"So I live off wholemeal bread and fresh fruit and vegetables. I get my protein from nuts and pulses, but I can still put weight on. So I do get enough to eat."

Trevor: "I suppose the vital question is - do you feel better after . . . what is it - a year of this?"

"I think I do. The question is how bad would I have felt if I hadn't done it. I think I do feel better on natural foods, anyway."

Trevor: "You watch the national press to keep abreast of the developments in this particular field?"

"Oh, yes. Although I am retired from nursing now, I still get the journals, and I still feel that I am a nurse. So I watch all the press and, if anything comes up that is relevant, I make enquiries and see if I can have a go."

Trevor: "Is this of benefit to other people with cancer? Do they ring you up?"

"Yes - all the time. Sometimes they just ring up for somebody to talk to. They know that I've had cancer, and that I've had radiotherapy. Sometimes they ring up and ask questions. They're probably going on a course of radiotherapy and they are a bit worried, or maybe the family rings up to ask how best they can support them. So I get lots of enquiries."

Trevor: "Are there people who are particularly distressed because they can't cope?"

"I have never had anyone distressed because they couldn't cope, but I have had relatives of people who were distressed and couldn't cope, and so I've tried to give a little bit of comfort to them."

Trevor: "Now this is an interesting point here because you yourself have coped with this. You are buoyant and on top of the world. How has it affected your family?"

"When I first had cancer I was a mum, and had a very good, supportive husband, three children of my own and four foster children and, at that time, my husband said to me: 'You have just got to get better because if I lose you I'll lose the children as well.' So I just had to get better. There wasn't any question of maybe you will, or maybe you won't. I had to get better to keep my children.

I told everybody I had cancer and, twelve years ago, if you told anybody that, they took two paces hastily away from you because there was this fear that cancer spread just by touching. So a lot of the taboo has gone out of cancer, and I think you must speak openly about it."

Trevor: "How did your children react to the operations, and to the fact that you couldn't do the things you might have done when you were full of energy?"

"It didn't seem to bother them at all. Children are very resilient you know. They were sorry for me and would do little jobs to show how much they loved me, and to help me, but then cancer didn't mean anything other than measles or something like that to them. It wasn't until they grew older that they've appreciated what kind of disease cancer is, and I wouldn't have it any other way."

Trevor: "They haven't at any time had any recriminations against life, or God, or Faith?"

"No - never. Not to me at any rate. They have been very supportive. Now they've all fled the nest except for the two youngest - they are eighteen and twenty - both fostered, both very much loved, and they are very supportive. Life has been easier because

132

of them."

Trevor: "I was just thinking that life, with just seven children, without cancer, would be not particularly easy, but to cope with the two! Did you really want seven children?"

"I did."

Trevor: "Like the old woman in the shoe?"

"That's what people used to say. We had three of our own, and then we took in four foster children whom we had permanently.

We had three foster children permanently for a long time, and we had lots of babies who came temporarily and when we got Danny, our fourth one, they said four is enough for anybody, and so we were restricted.

There were times, especially in the summer, when my husband would come home from work, and there would be two or three more faces at the tea table than were there at breakfast time.

It was just a way of living. We loved it. We lived in the country and it was a super place for children to grow up in, and we were a family who pulled together, and who all helped, so it was easier to raise seven than it would have been to raise one, I think, except when you got Christmas and birthdays. Then it was a financial strain, but you can't have everything can you?"

Trevor: "Some people want it, but whether you can get it is another matter. Lyn, we have talked about DOCATEF, and we have talked about your family. Let's talk about you, because what is it that makes you tick? How is it that you can live with this disease which, in your own case, you know hasn't stopped, and you are due for more surgery? How do you cope with this? Why aren't you bitter against life?"

"I suppose because I am an optimist. I have always been optimistic and, more so, I have always had a good sense of humour. If you can laugh at things it does help, so I think that's it in a nutshell."

Trevor: "There are many people who wouldn't find anything to laugh at in your situation. What would you find to laugh at when you think of what is happening to your body?"

"Well, you have only to look at yourself in the mirror first thing in the morning. I always say that, for someone who is not all there, I don't do too bad."

Trevor: "You can make a joke of that - the fact that you have lost a large proportion of your face which, to most women, is the piece that matters?"

"Fortunately I was never one of the types of ladies who used a lot of make-up, for instance, and laid a great store on my beauty. I was never a Helen of Troy - ever."

Trevor: "So apart from your optimism, there must be times when that deserts you, perhaps when you are feeling particularly weak, run down or something. When you have had a bad day. What happens to your optimism then?"

"It's still there, I've got a great faith as well, which is a comfort to me. I am not the only one who has suffered, you know. There are lots more who have suffered even worse than I have.

You have only got to look around you and you can find somebody in a worse situation than yourself any day of the week."

Trevor: "But that isn't always a comfort, is it, to know that there is suffering going on? If it's not you it will be someone else? I wouldn't find that a particularly attractive proposition. How do you cope with this? You say faith. What is this, faith in human nature, or faith in yourself?"

"No, faith in the Lord, I think. My faith means a great deal to me, more and more as life goes on, I think. I've got a good minister who is a good friend and, if I don't make it to church on Sunday, he will be round to see me in the week. I find him very supportive. We belong to a group of churches. I like the family service so I go to whichever church in the group has the family service that week, whether it is in Eastville, or Midville, Stickney, or Stickford. I'm prepared to go round in the group of churches, and I think my faith does help me a lot."

Trevor: "You find that being a member of the local parish church is a standby. You hear the Church of England being knocked for being out of date and useless, but you don't find that?"

"No, I don't. Most days I like to read my Bible. At first it used to be random, just picking up the book, but now I buy two booklets. *Every Day With Jesus* is one and *Daily Bread* is the other, which give me a text to read, and then they give me passages to read in the Bible and, nine times out of ten, it's relevant to today, to whatever is happening to me. I find it is a great help."

Trevor: "You can find relevance in the Bible, I suppose, Lyn, but has it never occurred to you to accuse God for making you like this?"

"Never."

Trevor: "Doesn't it seem unfair."

"Sometimes you think to yourself: 'Why has it happened to me?' But I would rather have had it happen to me than my husband or my children. I can cope with it personally, but if it happened to somebody I loved than I would probably resent it."

Trevor: "So there's a sort of paradox here, Lyn. It's alright for God to do it to you, but not to somebody else. Do you not see a flaw in the argument here, a fly in the ointment?"

"No, I don't. What about Jesus, God's son? It happened to Him didn't it? So I am just sharing the Lord's suffering."

Trevor: "So you feel in life there has to be suffering?"

"Oh, I think so. Ideally it would be different. Ideally there would be no Ethiopias. No suffering at all, but life is such that we have sometimes to accept these things. Some things we can fight against, join together and fight with, but some things you just have to accept."

Trevor: "So who is at fault for the Ethiopias, the cancers, the great diseases? Is it God, or man?"

"Well . . . I think a lot of it could be laid at man's

door, and then the elements don't help, do they? But I don't think I would blame God anyway, because if we all worked together we could eliminate a lot of things. For instance, all the money that goes on putting a man on the moon, it doesn't help you and me, does it?"

Trevor: "Not immediately."

"If that money was put to finding a cure for cancer it would save many many lives."

Trevor: "So you think life has got to be seen in proportion. That's the key is it?"

"That's right."

Trevor: "You used to live at, or at least the house used to be called, *The Kennels*, which confused me a bit when I started looking for it because the kennels have disappeared. You used to keep dogs, didn't you?"

"That's right, we did. We used to breed German Shepherds, commonly called Alsatians, and Yorkshire Terriers, and Labradors, but we used to board anybody's dogs while they went on holiday, from great big Pyrenean Mountain Dogs to tiny Yorkshire Terriers."

Trevor: "And this was simply because you liked dogs?"

"Yes, and my husband did too. Before that he was a gamekeeper - said the Lady Chatterley! But he did enjoy working with dogs."

Trevor: "You have always had something to do with bringing up children, or bringing up animals. What is this, a sort of love of creation?"

"Well, nature. Who can resist a child anyway?"

Trevor: "Or a puppy. What stopped you then . . . what put an end to your doggies?"

"Finance really. We just couldn't make it pay. When we first started there weren't many in the area, then, with the price of petrol increasing, I think people started looking for kennels nearer home, and who could blame them? We had our loyal ones and, when we did close down, we had some very tearful doggy owners saying that they wished we wouldn't close but, at the end of the day, there wasn't enough for the bread and butter, so we just had to give up."

Trevor: "You have had a go at children and dogs, and you are now about to bring out a record, I gather. Now tell us about that."

"Albeit reluctantly, because nobody has heard me sing yet have they?"

Trevor: "They could do now if you want them to."

"No thanks, Trevor. They are going to have to wait and pay for it. It evolved from a friend at Pilgrim Hospital, Eric Woods, who belongs to a group called Country Road. He said we ought to make a record and immediately we plumped for *One Day at a Time* for one side, but we couldn't think of anything for the other side. In August of last year I was in church at Stickford and Peter Lewis, the well-known modern hymn writer was there and, jokingly, I said to him 'You will have to write a hymn for the other side.' He took me at my word and he has written the words and the music of *Marvel at the Wonder*.

It is modern and it applies to every day that we have as it is now, and it's really nice. I am hoping that when it does come out people will buy it because its not for me personally, it's for Pilgrim. And for DOCATEF."

Trevor: "And the words are what?"

It's called **Marvel at the Wonder** and the first verse is:

Marvel at the wonder of creation,
  Everywhere God's loving hand is seen,
 Growing is a daily education,
   As we learn what living really means.

There are ten verses."

Trevor: "I think that first one sums up a lot of what you've been saying about creation and the wonder of it. It really is written for you."

"He did write it specially."

Trevor: "He seems to have summed you up in that verse."

"He even tells us:

Ponder how the earth and other planets,
Fly in space in orbits round the sun,
Galaxies that stretch minds to the limits,
God created every single one.

So it really is a hymn for today."

Trevor: "What would you say, Lyn, to someone who comes to you. They've just been, perhaps, to have a painful consultation with their doctor and they've just heard those words, however he phrases it, 'I am sorry, you have got cancer'? How would you advise a person to deal with that situation?"

"I would say to them that I am sorry you have got this trouble. You can't hide it, so you are going to have to learn to live with the fact that you have got cancer, and take every available thing that your doctors advise you, grab at anything, surgery or whatever, to get rid of it, but don't let it be the overriding thing in your life, and think you have got cancer so you cannot do this. With me, I like to do everything I want to do and cancer comes last.

You can't forget that you have got it, but don't dwell on it. At first I found it easier to talk about it, with my husband particularly, and my family, and get it off my chest. Talk to each other about it. You'll find that you will talk yourself out."

Trevor: "You don't try to hide it as many people do. We talk about cancer as Victorians used to talk about sex, that is you didn't say anything, or it was in hushed tones and behind closed doors. So you think you have got to bring it out into the open?"

"That's right, yes."

Trevor: "Now we have talked about your care for children, and for animals, but when you couldn't make animals pay, and you got rid of the children, you went on to another phase, didn't you, in mid-life. You went into nursing. What about that?"

"I had always wanted to be a nurse. When I was

a girl I grew up in Yorkshire where the main industry
was in the woollen mills, and then I had a back injury
and I had to go to work in a mill, while all the time
I really wanted to be a nurse.

And then suddenly I met Pat out of the blue.
We were pen pals at first and then I met him and all
I thought about was marriage and babies, so nursing
went out of the window.

Pat was really dead against me going out to work.
Then, to earn a bit of pin money I used to sell Tupperware.
I enjoyed going round to friend's houses selling it, and
then I got cancer. I had surgery in Boston and radiotherapy in Lincoln. I just got better from it and I wanted
a job and I didn't want to go back to Tupperware. So
I said to my husband 'I am going to apply to become
a nurse'. He laughed because, when the children cut
themselves, I used to faint at the sight of blood, but
I knew there were other things to being a nurse besides
being in an emergency where there was blood.

I knew I liked being with people so I applied.
Before I applied to be a nurse, I had applied at many
a store just to work behind a counter because I wanted
to work with people. Everybody rejected me when
they knew I had had cancer. So really I went to apply
to be a nurse thinking that if I got turned down I was
doomed. I had had so many rejections.

I made an appointment to see the Nursing Officer.
I went and had a word with her, and she was fantastic.
She didn't care that I had had cancer, and she helped
me fill my application form in.

She told me afterwards that, as I left the office,
she rang the surgeon and he fully approved of my nursing.

So, with his reference and my friend's reference,
I got the job as an auxiliary, and I enjoyed it so much
I told the Nursing Officer I would like to train to be
a nurse, but that I would prefer to be an auxiliary nurse
first to see if it really did appeal to me. So I started
as an auxiliary nurse on April 1st."

Trevor: "What year was that?"

"Oh, in 1973, and in November I started my training

to be a SEN and, again, I think I was very lucky because I nursed at the old hospitals, Wyberton West, London Road, and I started as an auxiliary at the White House Hospital, so I really appreciated Pilgrim Hospital when it came. I did most of my training at Pilgrim and when I qualified I went to Boston General Hospital to work as a geriatric nurse. (That's probably what I am now, but you know what I mean - a nurse working with geriatric patients). I really enjoyed that. If you work with geriatrics you notice that they always lift their face up and look at you, and are willing you to talk to them. They are like babies in a pram just waiting for somebody to talk to them. And if you have a smile and just a few words for them it can mean such a lot. Perhaps you remind them of someone, and I had such wonderful conversations with the old ladies."

Trevor : "You were enjoying this and then what happened?"

"I worked for nearly three years and then I decided to work nearer home and I went to The Gables at Spilsby. I had been there a week - I had just settled in - when, that night, as I was cleaning my mouth - I have to clean everything with not being absolutely normal - my tongue just chanced on a tiny lump.

I laughed to myself and thought I was being over sensitive and imagining things. I mentioned it to my husband and just laughed about it, put it out of my mind and, three weeks later, it was still there.

It was a Sunday evening and I had been on duty. I rang Pilgrim Hospital to see if the surgeon was going to be there. He was, and would see me, so I popped down to the hospital.

He looked at me and said, yes, it was a lump. He said I had better go into hospital the next morning and go into the theatre. I did, and the lump was malignant.

I had a major operation which lasted . . . I can't remember . . . I think it was four or five hours. It was a terrific operation. I had a tracheotomy and skin grafts and lost a lot of the framework of my face. And that is how it all started the second time, because

140

I had had five years' remission.

Everybody has been supportive. You go into Pilgrim Hospital, first as an outpatient and the ladies on reception were absolutely wonderful to me and, if ever I wasn't very well, there was always a seat found for me. They were very, very caring.

And then I saw the surgeon in his clinic and, again, the nursing staff and the surgeon were very caring.

You follow through by going onto the ward but I can honestly say, with my hand on my heart, I don't get any better treatment now than I got twelve years ago when nobody knew me. The care and the love and the attention is just the same. You can't get better than the best, and I rate Pilgrim very, very highly."

Trevor: "What of the future Lyn? You are always the optimist, so what of the future?"

"I get my rewards anyway just by seeing the surgeons' faces when you can present them with some new equipment. And, for instance somebody came up to me last week and said: 'DOCATEF gave my dad another two years. It extended his life, and we always feel that it was because of DOCATEF we had him for an extra two years.'

It's when people come and say things like that or 'They used the gastroscope on me the other week and, thank God, it was only an ulcer'... that's when I get my reward."

Trevor: "You too, can say thank God and you did want to Lyn, because you said you wanted to read a poem."

"This was given to me by a dear friend. I saw it on her mantelpiece and I said, 'Oh, I would like that' and last week, in the post, she sent it to me.

It's called **The Cross in my Pocket.** It's on a simple card and there's a little silver cross up in the right hand corner. It goes:

I carry a cross in my pocket
A simple reminder to me
Of the fact that I am a Christian
No matter where I may be.

This little cross is not magic
  Nor is it a good luck charm
It isn't meant to protect me
  From every physical harm.

It's not for identification
  For all the world to see
It's simply an understanding
  Between my Saviour and me.

When I put my hand in my pocket
  To bring out a coin or a key
The cross is there to remind me
  Of the price he paid for me.

It reminds me, too, to be thankful
  For my blessings day by day
And to strive to serve him better
  In all that I do and say.

It's also a daily reminder
  Of the peace and comfort I share
With all who know my Master
  And give themselves to His care.

So I carry a cross in my pocket
  Reminding no-one but me
That Jesus Christ is Lord of my life
  If only I'll let him be.

I think that's lovely . . ."

14.

TARGET - GREECE

I felt ill, very ill, in December 1984. Mr. Knowles suggested I wait until after Christmas before going into hospital for treatment after investigations proved that the cancer was active again and up to its old tricks. The delay in treatment suited me because daughter Patricia was coming home from Greece for the first time in nine years, and was bringing with her our grandchildren, Kathy and Patrick. I would be seeing Patrick for the first time.

For months I had been preparing for the visit, baking when I was well enough and filling the deep freezer and pantry with all kinds of goodies. But all too often I felt tired and became like a sloth. It tired me to climb the stairs and I would even delay going to the toilet because I couldn't face that climb. I sat in my chair all day, worn out, sometimes crying because I was ashamed of myself. I was always glad when Pat or Danny offered to prepare the meals. It was an offer that was never refused.

In the melancholy of this tiredness I decided that I had had enough. I would have no more surgery. It was time to give in. Time to end the fight. Cancer was winning. It was remorseless and grinding me down. The fight was over. Time for me to quit. I told my daughter Kathy that I'd had enough. She was shocked, sad, and upset, but said she understood.

I told Pat and the boys. They said I would feel better soon, and they became more protective. I became more dependent.

I went into Pilgrim Hospital for biopsies. The cancer,as I feared . . . as I knew . . . had spread. It had intruded into my lower jaw, deeper into my remaining cheek and higher into my orbital area. I had a blood transfusion and perked up after that. But I was still feeling low and unsure how to tell my diligent and trusty surgeon that I'd had enough and that the battle . . . his battle, and my battle . . . was over.

Every night I sat in my chair near the cooking range, seeking warmth, either reading or watching television. Whatever it was it was done half-heartedly, disinterestedly. If the telephone rang I hoped it was not for me. I was too tired to answer: did not want to talk.

One call, however, I did answer. It was from a dear friend, Audrey Hill. Audrey is not the type of person you ignore, however you might be feeling. I couldn't refuse to speak to her, as I had refused to speak to many other callers.

Audrey was a wholehearted supporter of DOCATEF, always full of fun and energy. A person I admire greatly. I told her of my fears and troubles. I wouldn't say she dismissed them because she is too sensitive and understanding for that, but her reaction was: "Of course you are going to fight it, Lyn. So many people depend on your courage."

I stayed silent. I never told her of the decision I had made.

Audrey laughed and continued: "You know what I mean, Lyn. People see how you cock a snook at cancer and they think if Lyn Ellis can do it so can they. Of course you are going to fight it." I found myself saying: "Of course I'm going to fight it, Audrey. I am going into Pilgrim Hospital after Christmas for more surgery."

She wished me luck and said she would visit me in hospital.

I went back to my chair and Pat remarked how much brighter I looked.

Christmas drew nearer and the excitement of the imminent arrival of Trish and her children was uppermost in my mind. The only worry was that she had asked us to meet them at the airport and, quite without thinking how we would do this, I had written back and agreed.

We told everybody about our family Christmas plans, including dear friend Bill Eason, from Toynton, who immediately offered to take me to Heathrow Airport on Christmas Eve to meet Trish. It was, he said, my Christmas present. I was knitting Bill a cardigan for Christmas. It seemed a poor exchange. As ever, with Bill and Auntie Millie, it was a fun drive and, in next to no time, it seemed that we were waiting for the arrival of the flight from

Greece. I brushed a stray hair from across my face, and I realised instantly that I had forgotten to put the patch over my eye. A little girl standing nearby looked me straight in the face and smiled gently as if to say "It doesn't look too bad."

We waited. An old Greek man emerged. From head to foot he was dressed in new clothes. He looked bewildered, lost and afraid, his face encased in a deep, fearful frown.

Suddenly, from the milling crowd, a lady of my own age cried "Here he is! Pa-pa! Pa-pa!" The old man looked up, the frown disappeared. His eyes sparkled and his whole face smiled. He put down his cases and stood with his arms outstretched. It was touching to see them embrace, good to hear snatches of Greek words which we had learned on holiday in Greece.

Other passengers came and went, and disappeared as they were joyfully claimed by waiting relatives. But no Trish and the children.

I felt weak and tired and leaned heavily on a barrier, and closed my one good eye. I was awakened by Trish's welcome voice calling 'Mum'. My tiredness forgotten, I pushed past the barrier and rushed to my little Greek family.

Little Kathy turned to Patrick and said "Nana". The little boy had seen only photographs of me, but held out his arms and he, too, called "Nana" and clung to me, putting his tiny arms around my neck.

My eye filled with tears of happiness.

The children were so well behaved on the journey home. Trish repeatedly put her arm around me and squeezed me to her. "I hope it snows," she said. "The children have never seen snow."

She was to get her wish. It turned very cold and snowed overnight. She and the children were thrilled and excited.

The journey had sapped my energy and I felt so tired. I sat in my chair, too weary to cuddle the children.

Daughter Kathy and son Garry came to visit their sister and, for the first time in nine years, almost the whole family was together. Just foster children Susan and David were missing. Susan was in Brighton and David in London.

Kathy asked if I would mind if Trish spent a few days with her, and Garry wanted her to stay with him. I was pleased because

I felt Trish's holiday was being spoiled by my tiredness, but sad because I wanted her all to myself.

On Christmas Day Auntie Millie rang to say Bill had been taken ill and had been admitted to hospital. He was worried because he couldn't take Trish back to the airport. Immediately I telephoned the hospital and asked the charge nurse to tell him not to worry, to get well soon and think of only himself for once.

The snow came again, thick and fast. Trish must have wished too hard.

Kathy's husband Nash took her and the children to Heathrow and it was only his driving skills which got them there on time.

Christmas over, it was back to Pilgrim Hospital and more surgery.

One of the visitors as I recovered was Audrey Hill. I told her that it was only because of her comments that I was back in hospital. She was thoughtful and apologetic and, although I laughed and said it was the best thing for me, I felt Audrey went home a little upset that night.

Later, I discovered, she commented to her mother: "What Lyn really wants is a good holiday with Pat. Wouldn't it be nice if we could send her on one?"

Next day she floated the idea to the Boston and Sleaford Target newspaper who, perhaps because they too found it difficult to say 'No' to Audrey, wholeheartedly supported the idea and launched the Lyn Ellis Holiday Fund, which I mentioned earlier.

No-one consulted me. Had they asked my permission I should have refused. I was grateful for all the support my fund had received and I knew that some people had been more generous than they could really afford. The only reward I needed was to hear surgeons and doctors say how much more quickly they had been able to detect and treat cancer because of the equipment that DOCATEF had bought.

One night, after a really painful day, Pat came to visit me in hospital. "When you are better, Lyn," he said, "I'm going to take you away for a holiday - anywhere in the world."

His eyes were brimming with tears as he held me closely and said "I do love you, Lyn."

I knew the state of our bank balance so I suggested that he

should take me to his brother David's house in Penrith.

"No, we can go further than that, my love." Then he told me about the holiday fund.

"Wouldn't it be super to visit our Trish," I murmured, hardly believing what I was saying, but remembering the cold Christmas and the pain, and the tiredness, and the grandchildren I longed to hold in my arms.

It was an outrageous, impossible, but lovely thought.

I was discharged at the weekend and couldn't wait to see the Target. The headlines shouted out: "Let's send Lyn on holiday."

Slowly I began to get better, and money rolled in from the Target appeal. Sheila Robson, another journalist friend at the Lincolnshire Free Press in Spalding, joined in the campaign, and friends I had made through DOCATEF organised fund-raising events.

Typical of the response was that of the landlord of one of Boston's pubs who insisted that money raised by his customers should help towards the holiday, and not, on this occasion, go to DOCATEF.

"She has done so much for us, now it is our turn to do something for her," was his attitude. It was all very touching.

It was soon apparent that there would be enough money for Pat and me to go to Greece, especially as Intasun - one of a number of holiday companies and major airlines to receive letters from Audrey - offered us free flights, and a fortnight in a hotel. We welcomed the flights, but declined the hotel because we wanted to stay with Trish, her husband and two children.

Boston travel agent Stephen Walker made the arrangements and appeared as excited as we were. Motor dealers Holland Brothers provided transport, and a chauffeur - Keith Harrison - for the journey to and from the airport.

Two weeks before the holiday I had two severe haemorrhages and had to go into Pilgrim Hospital for tests. Thankfully the report was good, but I was weakened. Nothing, however, was going to stop me from heading for Greece. A week before the departure I was allowed a spending spree at Mackays shop in Boston, after the official closing time, and bought things for myself and Pat and was not allowed to see the bill.

It was then that I really believed it was all happening.

There was, however, still one big problem. We were depending

147

our son Danny to look after the rabbit-farming business while we were away. He was the only one with the experience to feed the animals, and the only one familiar with the routines for taking them to market.

It was essential that he could drive - and he hadn't passed his driving test. He was taking the test just a few days before we were due to leave. I think Pat and I were more nervous than Danny.

When he returned from the test we watched his face for signs of which way it had gone. He was giving nothing away. Poker faced he walked slowly into the house. There was no hint until suddenly, he burst out smiling and yelled: "I did it Mum, you can go on holiday now."

We were given a champagne send-off by friends and Target staff and the ever-thoughtful Audrey had packed a hamper full of goodies to eat en route, flasks of tea and coffee for Pat and our superb driver, Keith Harrison, and wholemeal vegetarian sandwiches for me.

Keith was a tower of strength and made good time.

The young man at the reception desk at the airport was prepared for our arrival and, when other passengers left to board the plane in the airport bus, he took us to a private car. There were two passengers in it already, but they quickly volunteered to walk. As the man and young lady eased themselves out of the car, the man pulled on a peak cap, held out his hand and said "I am your captain."

At the plane the young man introduced us to the hostess, and we were shown to our seats.

We had to wait nearly an hour for take-off, and the rain blew coldly onto my face through the open door. I tried to protect it with magazines from the rack and the senior hostess, seeing my plight, did her best to shield me by standing in front of me. Yet the wind still blew cold and wet. It was a great relief when the door was finally shut and it was time for take-off. The flight was uneventful and it was 4.30 a.m. when we arrived in Athens. Now the air was warm and welcoming. Waiting at the foot of the steps was a young Greek man with a wheelchair and he whisked us through passport control.

Passing a floral display of bright red flowers, he plucked

one from their midst and said: "For you madam, welcome to Greece."

Pat collected our luggage and we sat in the main entrance waiting for Trish to collect us.

We sat for an hour and neither Trish nor George came, so we took a taxi to Argiroupolis. The driver was reluctant to take us and, it seemed, deliberately lost us. I was almost sick in his taxi as he sped up and down the streets, reversing angrily when neither of us recognised any landmark. Eventually, after a hair-raising hour of this, I recognised a building and, from there onwards could guide him to Trish's flat. The driver charged us 1,800 Dm - nearly eighteen pounds - and sped off into what was left of the night.

We walked up to the door to ring the bell which would tell Trish we were there, and which would open the door, but the sun had bleached away all the name tags. I pressed one bell and a female voice shouted down to us in irate Greek.

We decided not to try the others. It was now about 6.45 a.m. The air was lovely and warm. We sat together on the top of a flight of marble steps which had been bleached almost white by the hot sun.

My head ached. We were both tired. I started to cry quietly to myself. Pat put his arm around me and gave me a hug. We knew the factory where George worked started its machines at 7.30 a.m. and was close to the flats and workmen would be about soon.

Just after 7.00 a.m. the caretaker came down. He opened the door, speaking Greek. We both said "Georgio Pandazis" and the man pointed up the stairs. I went up in the lift and quickly we were at the door.

Trish answered it. Sleepily she asked: "Is it you, Mum?" and threw her arms around me. George hung his head in shame. They had overslept and were both terribly upset about it. They looked such a comical pair and couldn't believe it had happened. I laughed and said: "Don't worry. Things can only get better."

The children heard our excited chatter and got up to investigate.

Little Kathy flung her arms round my neck and, in broken English said: "I luvva you, Nana."

Pat opened the case with the presents in. It was just like Christmas. Then George had to go to work and Pat and I climbed into bed. We slept for a long time and, when I woke up, my head was in agony. I couldn't lift it off the pillow. I began to panic. I had no medical insurance cover because no-one would insure me. I was too big a risk.

I began to weep and Pat said: "Don't cry Lyn, it will make you worse."

I took two Diconal tablets and went back to sleep. Two hours later the pain woke me up again, so I took two more tablets. This time I didn't sleep but rested quietly in a darkened room.

The effect of the tablets lasted only two hours. As I stayed in bed, Trish blamed herself for not meeting us at the airport. We quickly assured her that the pain was because I sat in a draught before the take-off of the aeroplane. I stayed in bed for three days, taking the tablets every two hours. Then one night I slept all through and reduced the dosage to one tablet every six hours.

From that point onwards the holiday was enjoyable.

We went to the beach almost every day, except when a taxi strike restricted our sun bathing to Trish's balcony, and Pat enjoyed the sightseeing.

On the beach Pat insisted I put a towel on my head. "You mustn't get sunburned on your face," he said. I think it was because he did not want me to see him ogling the topless bathers!

The holiday was a tonic for me, relaxing on the beach and having family treats together. A day didn't pass, however, without thoughts of those kind people back in Lincolnshire - the people who had made it all possible.

And never a night went by without my thanking God for their love.

All good things must come to an end, they say, and it was certainly with mixed feelings that we left Greece. Sad to leave Trish and the children, who sobbed as we departed, but happy to return to our family and friends in England.

George took us to the airport and waited until we went through passport control. "Goodbye Mam and Dad," he said. "Come back soon. We love you."

We were allowed on the plane first and, this time, sat in its warmth and sunshine.

On the flight back we ordered drinks but were not allowed to pay for them. "With the compliments of the staff" we were told. "Because we admire your courage and desire to help others."

Ten out of ten for Audrey – yet again.

15.

INTO 1986
- DAY BY DAY

I LOVE CHRISTMAS. Or, more correctly, I used to love Christmas with the fun, the preparations, and the family together. More recently I have become wary of it because Christmas has coincided with the time of the year when a new cancer-induced trauma has occurred in my life.

All over Christmas 1985 I felt uneasy. Never far from my mind was the thought that perhaps it would be my last one . . . I felt tired, almost weak.

On Christmas Eve my friend Corinne Ness telephoned to ask if I still wanted to attend Midnight Mass at Boston Parish Church (The Stump). "Yes please." I was thrilled at the idea.

Corinne insisted that I wear her mother's fur coat. I felt as if I had won the pools. For many years I had wanted to attend Midnight Mass at the Stump and when the service started my legs were trembling and shaking. I took communion, taking the bread and wine from Fred Moss, definitely one of my favourite people. Thanks to Corinne, and her son Martin who drove us to church, it was one of my best Christmas Eves.

Christmas Day and Boxing Day were spent with the family, but I felt listless and tired, very tired. I didn't feel any less tired as the holiday passed. I was due to end the year with yet another stay in Pilgrim Hospital.

On the last Monday of the year I waited for my friendly vicar Robin to give me an early morning lift to the hospital in his Landrover. It was very cold and the windows were frozen over. I couldn't have anything to eat or drink. I needed a painkiller but knew, too, that was impossible.

I began to shiver uncontrollably. Pat filled a hot water bottle for me and I sat waiting with my big coat and scarf on. The pain in my face increased and I began to cry. I had difficulty in climbing into Robin's Landrover when he arrived, and I was sad and lonely when I arrived at Ward 2B at Pilgrim. No-one else was there. All patients and staff had been concentrated on Ward 2A over Christmas. But slowly the old routine began to emerge and I sat in the day room awaiting the call. The porter who wheeled me into the anaesthetist's room joked that I must have put on pounds in weight over Christmas.

I woke up in the recovery room and remember nothing about being taken back to the ward. I slept on and off during the afternoon, before Mr. Knowles came in with disturbing news. There were two lesions in my right lung. He thought about half of the lung was involved.

It came as a great shock. I'd had the X-ray more than two weeks earlier and I'd assumed that no news was good news. It wasn't. Now I knew why I had been so very tired and lethargic. Mr. Knowles went on to say that he'd removed slivers of bone – the purpose of the latest operation – and was awaiting a report from the pathologist, but he feared this would show further cancer involvement in my face and head.

I asked what action was planned. Had he heard from Professor Dumonde about whom I had spoken to him some time earlier?

I had happened upon the name of Professor Dumonde and his work while watching a news item on television. He had been working on a new vaccine for the treatment of cancer, my kind of cancer, in the nose, cheek, and jaw. The breakthrough had taken place at Bristol and Manchester Universities. It had been tested on animals with a good success rate. Now the doctors were ready to try it out on patients.

As I thought more and more about the new vaccine, and about offering myself as a guinea pig, I remembered the television journalist, Suzie Collette, who had interviewed me for an I.T.N. programme. I telephoned and asked her if she could find out more about the news item.

Late the following day she rang to say that the man in charge of the project was Professor Dudley Dumonde and he was based at St. Thomas' Hospital, London. The drug was Interleukin No 2.

Immediately I had telephoned Mr. Knowles and he had agreed to try to contact the professor. Now here I was back in hospital and wondering if Professor Dumonde had the solution to my problems. I couldn't believe that it was all happening again. My forehead itched and when I rubbed it the response was almost pleasureable pain. I couldn't leave it alone.

The doctors and nurses were again a great comfort. Pat had telephoned asking about me. He was always reluctant to visit on the first night after an operation, but he had asked the nurse if I could ring him back when I felt fit enough.

When I rang, Stephen answered the 'phone, but, after asking "Are you all right, Mum?" he quickly passed me over to his dad. I was pleased to get away without having to say a great deal to Stephen.

In these circumstances I always felt sorry for Pat, caring and worrying alone. I could sense his disappointment again - a disappointment not for himself but for me. But the pay-phone devoured the coins and ended our conversation.

During the night there was a noisy emergency admission which woke me up and, try as I might, I could not find sleep again. My face and head were hurting and itching. Although at first it was soothing to massage my forehead gently with my fingers the pleasure soon turned to pain. My finger tips were bloody. I had chafed the skin away.

The duty doctor increased my painkiller dosage but dawn had passed before I fell to sleep. In the morning I felt weary and still desperately tired after being awakened and having washed.

Mr. Knowles came in and, from the look on his face, I knew he was bringing bad news.

"I have been looking at your X-ray report," he began. "There are unfortunately two more spots . . . "

This was an unexpected blow. I had the complete answer to why I had been so tired and feeling so lazy. I thanked Mr. Knowles for his frankness. What a way to end 1985!

It hadn't been a very healthy year, and things were not looking good for 1986.

My face and head were hurting and I rang the bell to ask if it was time for more painkillers.

One nurse, Pam Blackburn, brought my tablet, and sat on my bed. I squeezed her hand. "Thanks", I said. Lucy Potter, the auxiliary nurse, came in. She hadn't heard my news. She held my left hand. I tried to speak, but I didn't know what to say. A big tear rolled down my cheek on to my nightie . . . Anyway, I decided, cancer wasn't going to come between me and my food, so I enjoyed my tea when it came. I am a vegan so Sister had arranged for my meal to be salad with jacket potato.

It wasn't long before Pat arrived, alone. Another visitor soon to follow was Wendy, the Sunday School teacher from the Stump, who brought me a card from the children, and then, like a breath of fresh air, Audrey Hill breezed in, looking like a model from Vogue.

Audrey and Wendy left together after about half an hour. Pat moved his chair nearer. We sat and held hands. I felt sleepy. Pat left and I dozed off. When I woke the night nurses had taken over.

I had another restless night. At 4.00 a.m. I walked into the day room to join the nurses there and had a glass of sherry and a piece of Christmas cake. It was New Year's Eve!

New Year's Day and Pat and Danny visited me. I watched Pat's face when we were alone. Thinking I was asleep, he gazed towards me. His eyes were large and full of unshed tears. I love him so much and wanted to make him smile. He reached out and held my hands. We each knew only our own thoughts. I must get better and not leave him alone.

He is very much a loner, content with nature and God's gifts of spring, summer, autumn, and winter; but he needs life and laughter - and love too. That is something very special which we share. Pat has always been my best friend and shunned the company of others, satisfied and happy with his lot, ready to share his last penny, doing his own work and helping me when the chores get too much.

"There's no need for you to do that," he would say when he saw me struggling. "You just rest and get better."

He can now bake, sew, and do the ironing.

Sometimes I feel guilty when I enjoy the company of friends, and he is at home, on his own.

He promised to support me when I started the fund. He has been true to that promise. "But please don't ask me to attend functions," he implored. I have tried to accept that part of the deal, too.

From time to time I look at friends of my own age, some of them nurses following their profession full-time. One of my biggest regrets has been having to give up nursing. I envy those who have been able to carry on.

Some of my friends enjoy dancing and sport. I envy their energy and talent. Yet, strangely, I have had a good, satisfying life. I have managed to do things that others, fit and well, have not achieved. Most important, I have been loved and cherished, and been helped to help others . . . cancer patients . . . and, perhaps, have helped to save a few lives.

Truly, I have not had cancer for nothing.

As the first day of 1986 came to an end I sat talking to the senior nurse on duty, Pam Pearl. We had worked together eleven years ago. Suddenly there was a crash in the corridor. A patient had fallen. Pam was out and in control in a flash, as if following text book procedure. I enjoyed listening to her demands of the junior nurses.

January 2nd 1986: I woke up in pain at about 4.00 a.m. I rang for the nurse. Joan, the auxiliary, came; she returned to Pam Pearl and, together, they counted out the Diconal. Because it is a 'dangerous drug' each tablet has to be accounted for.

They returned to my ward, checked my identity, and gave me one Diconal - plus, at my request, a cup of hot mint tea.

I was very tired and fell asleep almost as they left, to wake again at about 7.30 a.m. As usual I was in pain. My face was hurting more than ever and I lifted my hand to comfort it. In my anguish I didn't see the nurse leave, but she was quickly back with another Diconal.

The familiar sounds around me - the linen skip, wheelchairs in the corridor, nurses' chatter, the morning report - all reminded me of the days when I was dishing out the sympathy and help; today I was on the receiving end, and glad of the super nurses on call.

Dr. Vince Cumberworth visited me. He was interested in the work of Professor Dumonde and, the previous night, had prepared a summary of my case to send to St. Thomas's. He thought the case most interesting.

As the doctor was about to leave, the phlebotomist (the lady who takes blood samples) arrived to take a sample of mine.

We have known each other a long time and she has taken many samples of my blood during our twelve years' association with the Pilgrim Hospital. She struck lucky first time and extracted my blood into a syringe and placed it in two phials. The blood looked darker and I was pleased. It looked as if it had plenty of iron in it: but if it proved that I was anaemic I would be having a blood transfusion. Alarm bells rang, and I thought of AIDS!

But I didn't voice my fears.

Having a Diconal tablet every four hours was beginning to do the trick and keep me pain free. As ever, DOCATEF was not far from my mind and secretary, Noreen Evison, popped in for a chat to sort out some fund business.

Pat and Stephen, who had been to market, called in late afternoon. A visit at this time saved them the petrol of a return journey into Boston from Eastville and, in their wake, came Mr. Knowles and a retinue of doctors and nurses.

Mr. Knowles examined my forehead. I had rubbed the skin off and it looked a mess. Turning to a junior doctor he requested that the allergy be reported in my notes and prescribed an ointment for it.

I was disappointed when Pat and Stephen had to go, as I wasn't expecting visitors that evening. I read a little and then fell asleep. I was surprised that it was nearly midnight when I woke up. My face and head were hurting, and my back was painful too. The nurse hadn't awakened me for my 6.00 p.m. Diconal because, she said, I looked so peaceful in sleep.

I was wide awake now, however, so I studied my Bible a little. My hair was irritating me. It is so long that, about every three months, I have the urge to get it cut. I can't afford perms and regular hair 'dos' so I keep it long. I can't find a hairdresser in the hospital salon who is happy to set my hair. Perhaps they all think my face would upset and scare off their other customers. I can't blame them!

It proved to be a restless night.

January 3rd 1986. During the long hours of sleeplessness I had been wondering if the tumour in my chest was a new primary or another secondary, and reminded myself to ask Mr. Knowles. The nurse gave me two tablets of Voltarol, and I reached into my locker for my daily selenium and yeast tablets. I feel better for taking these every day. My sight is bad this morning. Perhaps I am tired from the drugs.

I enjoyed the luxury of a bath but dozed for most of the day, between meals and visitors. I tried to write my diary but kept falling asleep in mid sentence. The terrible spelling and writing were proof of my barely conscious state.

Dr. Cumberworth came back for another sample of blood for a serum test. I was to have a pint of blood in the morning.

After the afternon drinks my Pat came visiting alone; the boys had gone into town to do the shopping. I was able to tell him that I was going home on Monday, my forty-ninth birthday.

He said it was snowing in Eastville, and I was in the best place in hospital – certainly the warmest.

We had only enough coal left at home to last five days, he said. It was a difficult time financially, and we usually received the telephone and electric bills during the first week in January. Pat said not to worry, something usually turns up.

Mr. Knowles came in at about this time. He was concerned that I was not getting pain relief and wanted to try another drug. I wasn't too keen on changing and said I would prefer to have one Diconal every three hours. I requested not to have too many pain killers because I preferred to suffer some pain rather than be drowsy or sleeping all the time. In the end he left the choice to me.

The drowsiness continued for the rest of the day.

January 4th. I had slept well and without pain. At about 9.00 a.m. Dr. Cumberworth came into my room to carry out the blood transfusion. He found a good vein and, with ease, pushed in the needle and attached a bottle of normal saline. He told me I would be getting two packs of blood cells. I can go home tonight.

Every half hour my temperature and pulse were taken, as well as my blood pressure. I felt so tired . . . . and went to sleep.

Pat came visiting with Garry. It was lovely to see them. My arm began to ache with the strain of the blood transfusion, and my temperature began a steady climb. I finished one pack of blood cells and normal saline was introduced until the next pack of blood arrived.   My blood pressure was normal.   My temperature just fluctuated.   With the second pack in situ I could only sit and wait.

Mr. Knowles came.   He was pleased I was free of pain, and said I could go home tomorrow.   Visitors came and went but when I was left on my own the pain became intolerable.   The second pack of blood had run through and a pack of normal saline went up.   I went to the toilet and turned a bit funny, but said nothing, cleaned my mouth and climbed back into bed.

Sister said the drip could come down.   I couldn't believe that sticking plaster held down the canula as I had declared that I was allergic to elastoplast.   Now my arm was red and patchy. I began to cry, gently at first and then in big bucketfuls.

Sister, on a medicine round, insisted that I took two Diconals. She watched me swallow them and remonstrated: "You are not doing yourself any good by being too brave."

I was so cold, and trembled.   Someone filled my hot water bottle and Sister wrapped me up well.   I refused supper when it came and snuggled down.   I cried myself to sleep.

I slept for about five hours, then made a couple of 'phone calls and read both local newspapers.   There was a picture of me accepting money for DOCATEF in both of them.   I started to write my diary, but my writing was awful.   I felt ashamed.

I began to feel hot and sweaty.   My arm was red and bloody where the plaster had been.   Nurse Peggy took my temperature and it was far too high.   I began to drink cold water and the pain came back.   I was given a Diconal and tried to get to sleep, but I began to feel hot - a rare experience for me.   I threw back the blankets but became hotter and hotter.   Peggy re-made my bed with cool linen and suggested a cool wash down.

I knew all this was my body's reaction to the transfused blood but, after the bed bath, I started to feel almost right again, and I fell asleep almost as soon as I had had another Diconal.

. January 5th 1986.   I awoke at about 6.00 a.m.   The pain in my head and cheek was there again.   Nurse fetched me another Diconal and gave me another blanket as I was feeling chilly.   I settled down and went to sleep again.

I am a slow eater and it took a long time to eat my breakfast although I hadn't eaten since midday the previous day.

Bill came to fetch me home in the afternoon. The wind outside felt cold and sharp, and whipped round my face.

It was good to be home. 'Efel' was throwing out lots of heat. I sat in my usual spot and read the paper. Stephen cooked tea. I cheated and opened some of my birthday presents. I was pleased with the leg warmers.

I went into the bathroom and, for the first time since the operation, I could examine my mouth. I noticed two lumps had gone, and when I gently swabbed, although the area turned bright red as the blood rushed to the surface, it didn't bleed.

I felt cold despite the new electric blanket when I went to bed. Pat cuddled me until I was warm and fell asleep.

January 6th 1986. My birthday. I'd forgotten, but Pat reminded me with a 'Happy Birthday' as I awoke. He dressed and came to my side of the bed to kiss me, went downstairs and returned with my tablets and a cup of mint tea. And a birthday card from him.

I thanked him for the lovely card. His eyes were full of tears. We kissed. He looked so sad and sorry. I could almost read his thoughts: "Will this be her last birthday?"

I said: "Don't cry my love. When I've been to London I'll be better . . . cured. This time next year I'll be back nursing."

He brushed aside his tears and went downstairs to get his breakfast. He returned with a handful of cards, and then the telephone started ringing with birthday wishes.

I decided to get up, went into the bathroom and cleaned my mouth. Again no haemorrhage, and I realised that I had gone about eight hours without Diconal. I was very pleased with myself.

Pat remarked how well I looked after the transfusion. The blood, he said, had most probably been donated by a meat eater, not a vegan.

I opened my cards, took 'phone calls and had a quiet day. Pat and Stephen cooked the tea. I became upset because the room looked untidy, and started to tidy up. I went into the dining room to find biscuits and cake to offer friends who had called. All I could find were three crummy biscuits going soft in a tin.

If only I felt well, I could so easily bake and ice a few fairy cakes. I felt so frustrated and began to cry again. Stephen and Pat helped with the tidying. I was more upset because I needed their help.

I went upstairs to have a good cry on my own and I lay on the bed and sobbed.

Stephen shouted upstairs "Mum, you are wanted on the 'phone."

"I'm not speaking to anyone," I shouted back.

I heard Stephen return to the living room, and then re-trace his steps. Mum, Mum, it's our Trish."

I pushed my hair out of my face, wiped my nose and eye with a tissue, took a deep breath and picked up the telephone.

She knew I was crying, but I lied and told her I had just had a row with her Dad. I didn't want her to think I was crying because of the pain, or because I was so ill again.

But, as always, I told her the truth about my recent diagnosis, and had a quick chat with the children before she had to ring off.

I had a wash, brushed my hair, and went downstairs. The room looked tidier . . .

January 7th 1986. More birthday cards. Now I have thirty-six. More 'phone calls and visitors. One of the visitors was an old nursing friend, Polly Banham. "How old are you, Lyn?" she asked. "Forty-eight or forty-nine?"

"Forty-nine," I answered.

January 8th 1986. Our thirty-first wedding anniversary. I noticed a difference when I got up. I didn't cry with cold or pain. I am tolerating pain better. Only one Diconal all day. More birthday and anniversary cards, and a bouquet from friends, the Ireland family.

January 13th 1986. I went to Pilgrim Hospital to keep an appointment with Mr. Knowles. I had a blood test, and received a list of dates for further appointments. I felt ill after tea. My back ached and I was cold and shivery. Stephen filled my hot water bottle. I felt tired and my face hurt. I fell asleep clutching the bottle.

161

- - -

Every other day I rang Mr. Knowles' secretary, Shirley, to ask if she had heard from St. Thomas' Hospital in London.

- - -

The engagements to collect money raised for DOCATEF were coming in again, and I was able to resume the business of receiving cheques.

- - -

January 24th 1986.   At last a meeting with Mr. Knowles to hear of his talks with Professor Dumonde.   They'd had a long chat and he said I was not to raise my hopes about going to St. Thomas'. The treatment wasn't simple like giving an injection.   The white cells had to be collected and treated, and then introduced back into the body.

It had to be introduced at an artery or vein near the tumour, difficult to do in my case as I had had so much surgery.   There was a danger that it could go to the brain.

It couldn't be re-introduced through any old vein or artery otherwise it would undermine the whole immune system.   Did I understand?

Miserably, I said I did.   It could create an effect like AIDS.

"Exactly", said Mr Knowles.

"But what about my lung?"

"Just leave it," advised Mr. Knowles.   "Yours is such a slow growing tumour.   You've already had one thoracotomy; you can't keep having them."

It was possible to remove the lung, he said, but he advised leaving things for the time being.

Mr. Knowles examined my face when Pat told him I was taking more Diconal, and he thought more surgery could reduce the pain. He would make enquiries, and could I make another appointment to see him on Monday, February 3rd.

That was it.   End of the appointment.   End of me, it seemed.

During the night I afforded myself a weep.   I thought Pat was asleep until I felt his arm holding me close.   Neither spoke. And neither slept.

January 25th 1986.   There was a surprise.   Kathy and her

children arrived on a visit. The previous day she had telephoned to say her car had broken down and she could not make it. That had been a disappointment, but the car had been repaired and here she was.

The arthritis in my knee meant I could only wobble my way to the bathroom and I had to hold the wall to steady myself.

I began to clean my mouth and Kathy came looking for me. It was the first time she had seen me without my obturator since I'd had my eye removed. She watched as I syringed in the socket, peered in and said: "It's beautiful and clean, and much easier for you now."

Just then I must have caught a weak spot and blood began to pour down my nose and out of my mouth. Kathy looked alarmed. I put my obturator in. It presses against the bleeding part and stops it.

I was cleaning my face when young grandson Stuart poked his head round the bathroom door. He looked shocked. "It's nothing," I said. "Just Nana's funny face."

He nodded his little head seriously, as if he fully understood, and quietly closed the door.

– – –

As January trod its wintry path I tried to do without the pain-killers as much as possible, and life alternated between depression, brighter times, and pain.

– – –

February 3rd 1986. Another trip to Pilgrim Hospital and an appointment with Mr. Knowles. But first, on arrival there, I had a chat with a nurse who had been at the hospital for the whole of the twelve years I had been visiting. "I want another twelve years at least," I told her.

"Then you will be able to bring champagne again," she smiled.

I did not feel well enough to celebrate at that moment, but she had reminded me of a previous occasion when I did.

That had been seven years ago. I had asked for the last appointment of the day so that I could take a bottle of champagne to celebrate five years free from cancer.

163

I was nursing at Boston General Hospital at the time and the then nursing officer, Mrs. Beryl Johnson, had told me I could only take the drink if I was the last patient of the day.

I had taken two bottles and Mr. Knowles had offered to take the cork out of the first one. I agreed because, if anything went wrong, it would look better to have his name on the accident book than mine!

Mr. Knowles said: "Hopefully you've made it, Lyn. Don't come back for six months".

The euphoria had lasted three months. At the end of that time I went back to have my biggest operation – the maxillectomy.

There was no euphoria today, either. I reported to Pat, waiting in the car, that I had no news.

February 4th 1986. I woke up at 8.30 a.m. feeling well and fresh. I would surprise the men today and make a steamed treacle pudding and perhaps go to the Women's Institute meeting tonight. I set about making the pudding. Pat peeled the potatoes and I prepared the brussels, and cooked the tea. It was magic doing it by myself . . . until my back and head started, at first to have a niggling pain, and then a raging ache. Stephen took over the cooking.

I felt awful and rang my friend to apologise that I couldn't make it to the W.I. meeting.

February 6th 1986. I was depressed on waking and lay in bed in pain wondering what the hell I could do. I remembered my investment of £1,000 due to be released in April. That was from my Health Service pension fund. On impulse I rang Shirley, Mr. Knowles' secretary, and requested that she ask him if I could go abroad in search of treatment. Maybe China where, I understood, my type of cancer seemed to be more prevalent. She agreed to ask him.

Immediately afterwards I felt guilty. I'd as good as promised Pat half my money to expand his rabbit breeding business. He came in and found me crying. I told him what I had done and he was amazed. Or at least he looked it. He said that the money was mine to use as I wanted. Perhaps he would have given up the rabbits by April.

He sat on the bed stroking my head to ease the pain. "Don't cry Lyn," he said. Don't worry about the rabbits and money. You come first. I love you." He held me close.

164

The telephone rang.   It was Mr. Knowles.   He had heard from Professor Dumonde and did not hold out hope of finding anyone to treat, or operate, on me.

What about seeking treatment abroad?   I would need about £10,000 just for an opinion, he said.

"I've got relatives in Hong Kong."   I was almost defiant. "Intasun gave me free flights to Greece.   I could ask an airline to take me to Hong Kong.   It's worth a try."

Mr. Knowles did not seem very keen.

I apologised for troubling him.   He said it was no trouble – but said I should not raise false hopes.

Why did I have to have such a rare tumour?   Well, I'm not giving up.   This morning I was tempted to increase my dosage of Diconal and sleep my days away.   But not now – I felt I must continue the fight.

With a bit of detective work in the family I discovered the address of Uncle Jack, my mother's brother, who lived in Hong Kong.   He had, apparently, retired from the police force and worked for an airline.   It was a difficult letter to write and I was pleased when it was finished.

I cried myself to sleep.   I was worried about Pat.   He could not manage without my allowances.

February 7th 1986.   I was up early and surprised Pat.   I tidied the lounge.   When Stephen and Garry came home from work they remarked about the letter addressed to Hong Kong.   Garry said he would help me raise the £10,000 if I could go to China. . I begged them not to tell anyone outside the family and told them I would have another two years to live anyway.   I don't know why I said this; just to re-assure them, I suppose.

I've had twelve years since it was discovered I had cancer; I want another twelve years.

February 8th 1986.   I felt stifled and shut in.

February 10th 1986.   My vicar, Robin, came to visit and reminded me of the Rev. Ron File, now Vicar of Friskney, who had just returned from cancer counselling in Hong Kong.   He offered to get in touch, but I declined the offer until I had spoken to Mr. Knowles.

165

Robin said a prayer for me, and we said the Lord's Prayer together.

February 12th 1986. I saw Mr. Knowles at a DOCATEF committee meeting and told him about the Rev. Ron File. "Give him a ring," he suggested. "What have you to lose?"

February 13th 1986. The Rev. Ron File answered my call of the previous day, and listened as I asked if he knew any cancer specialists in Hong Kong. When he said he did not think there was anyone who could help, it was like a smack in the face. He offered aid through counselling, but I wanted more.

How could he help? I'd lived with, and fought, cancer for twelve years. I knew the score and was not afraid of dying!

Ron said he might be able to stop the spread of the tumour by fighting it from within. It was, he said, possible to control our bodies to fight disease. I would need help from my family, surgeon, and vicar.

I agreed to make an appointment to see him. Pat wasn't keen on the idea, but I felt sure he would go with me to try to help.

February 14th 1986. I was still in bed when Pat came up with a beautiful bouquet. "Who's sending you flowers?" he demanded. But his sheepish grin gave him away. I knew how hard up he was and it must have been a sacrifice to buy me flowers on Valentine's Day.

It reminded me of my last Valentine's Day as a nurse when, working on the ward at The Gables Hospital, in Spilsby, I was surprised to receive a beautiful bouquet. The quietly romantic Pat had sent them, and I had been the envy of all my colleagues and the old ladies in hospital.

Pat had this year also bought me a beautiful card, but I had forgotten it was Valentine's Day. Hastily I looked through my pile of cards and found a funny one that I'd forgotten to send a year ago.

Opening it, he remarked: "I'm sure I've seen this one before".

Eirwen called to take me to the DOCATEF dance being held in Alford. It was a nightmare journey because of the snow and ice, and blocked roads prevented many people from attending, but they insisted I had the £70 raffle money for the fund.

We travelled a different route home, slowly and safely, and

it was nearly 1.00 a.m. when we arrived home. Pat was waiting and came out to the car to help me into the house so that I didn't fall. He'd got the water hot for a bath. When I got inside I collapsed, but gradually pulled myself together. I looked into the mirror and was almost white. I slept well, after a slow start.

February 15th 1986. I sold £68 worth of raffle tickets at Pilgrim Hospital. I assured Pat I was well enough to do it, and felt better for having gone out the previous night.

February 16th 1986. With help from friends sold nearly another 100 books of raffle tickets at Pilgrim Hospital and, while there, had a chat with Dr. Bexton about the possible operation being discussed to ease the pain in my cheek. I was having reservations, as I told him, because, if he blocked the nerves and took away the pain, I would have no warning if the cancer were spreading. He agreed that was possible.

Also now I took only half a Diconal painkiller every six hours and this gave me a boost. Without it I might need something like Valium and I was reluctant to start taking drugs of that nature.

He promised to have a chat with Mr. Knowles, but wanted some X-rays of my bone structure.

Later I also had a chat with Mr. Knowles who reminded me: "Don't forget to have your blood tested. You are looking very pale."

Before leaving Pilgrim I visited a friend, Jimmy Lowis, who was a patient on the eighth floor. His wife Joan was there and she told me she had a collection of pennies for my fund. They are a wonderful couple. Both have been married before, and both lost their previous partners through cancer. When they married they requested donations to DOCATEF instead of wedding presents and were delighted to hand over nearly £700.

February 17th 1986. I got up just after midday and had a long bath. It was a mistake. I felt dreadful and sat in my chair for much of the day with a bad headache. I reasoned that it could have been just an ordinary, everyday headache.

In the evening we watched television and the telephone rang at ten minutes past ten. Rather late, we thought. Pat answered it and came back to say: "It's the Mayor of Boston." My legs went to jelly and butterflies floated around my stomach. I tried to think if I had done anything wrong!

The Mayor, Coun Alf Goodson, apologised for the lateness of the call, but he had just been to a meeting and he wanted to break the news himself.

Boston Borough Council had decided to give me, Lyn Ellis, the Freedom of the Borough! It was the council's ultimate honour, and given very sparingly and it was a unanimous decision by the councillors, said the Mayor.

I burst into tears and could hardly reply.

Pat and Stephen were astounded, and Stephen rushed upstairs to tell Garry.

I had a glass of sherry to celebrate.

That night I had a bad haemorrhage. I had great difficulty in getting off to sleep. It was the same for Pat.

February 18th 1986. When I woke up I thought I had been dreaming about the Freedom, but an early telephone call from Councillor Dr. John Wallis confirmed the reality of it all with his congratulations. Calls from newspapers, radio, and television added any more confirmation I needed.

It was bewildering.

Later in the day Pat and I had our first appointment with the Rev. Ron File, at Friskney. I was very nervous and edgy, but he said he felt sure he could help me. He would teach me how to get inside my body and deal with the tumours with my body's own defence mechanism.

Ironically that interview took place in the very same room where DOCATEF had had 'lift-off', when the then vicar of Friskney, the Rev. Bill Hurdman, persuaded me to speak to his parishoners at a coffee evening.

In the evening I watched myself on television!

February 19th 1986. More television and Press calls, and a radio interview. I also went to Pilgrim Hospital for the requested blood tests and X-rays. And I watched myself on television again at night. A friend from eighteen years ago rang to see if it really was me on 'the box' and another cancer patient telephoned with congratuations.

Pat insisted that I take a rest which I did until Eric Woods came at 9.00 p.m. to rehearse our planned record. When he left,

I wrote to the Foreign Affairs Minister seeking details of cancer specialists in China and Hong Kong.

Pat's brother David returned Pat's call, and said the family had never stopped praying for me.

I went to bed shattered but, for once, it was a healthy tiredness, and I fell asleep within minutes.

February 20th 1986. It was exciting to read the front page news about my Freedom in the Lincolnshire Standard and the Boston and Sleaford Target.

February 25th 1986. Pat and I had an appointment with the Rev Ron File at 1.30 p.m. to start the counselling proper. I had to relax and take deep breaths to fill my lungs to capacity. Just as I felt I might drop off to sleep, Ron told me to keep my eye shut and imagine that I was a tiny, minute Lyn. He led me into my lung and then into my head. I had to describe the tumours and try to move them. At one stage he said "Pick up a scalpel and cut them out".

But I couldn't. I told him everything had gone dark. He said: "take a big breath and breathe in light" and, strangely, I could see round the lung again.

After an hour he told me to open my eye when I felt like it. When I did he asked me if I could remember anything and what did it feel like.

"Yes," I said, "I remembered everything like a strange dream." He said that was good and I was to practise 'travelling' during the week, and he asked Pat to help me.

We were there for an hour and a half and I felt exhausted. I was worn out and slept for most of the evening.

February 27th 1986. Had terrible toothache which kept me awake all night.

February 28th 1986. I had toothache for most of the day but I went to Kirton to accept over £300 for DOCATEF. Photographer and television cameraman Bob Whitaker was there and bought me a whisky and lemonade. It took the toothache away and I slept like a log.

Those trips to the Rev. Ron File were a new, and interesting, experience for me. He tried to help me make my body resist the invasion of cancer, and taught me self-hypnosis to help me cope with the pain.

Only rarely, and then usually because I had brought up the subject, did we discuss God. Ron said he was sure it was not God's wish that I had cancer, but he offered no explanation why I'd got the damned thing.

As autumn 1986 brought a glorious 'Indian summer', I went back to Pilgrim Hospital for more laser surgery.

Shortly before I was due to receive the Freedom of the Borough of Boston I went on one of those now regular drives with dear friends Bill, his wife Evelyn, and Auntie Millie. Again it was an early start - and this time the destination was the City Hospital, Nottingham.

Everywhere we go the ladies are won over by Bill. He calls them all 'lovey' or 'sweetheart'. In Southampton the surgeon mistook him for my husband; a nurse asked if he was my Dad; and the Sister thought he was my fancy man!

After X-rays, blood tests, and a chat with the surgeon, Mr. Salama, and three house doctors, I was told I was to have a bronchoscopy and a lung scan.

I was taken by taxi to the Queen's Medical Centre in Nottingham. There was already one patient in the X-ray room when a porter left me opposite the room where the scan pictures being taken appeared on a screen.

I was fascinated watching the pictures until a young man came up and said: "You are not supposed to be there, Mrs. Ellis."

It surprised me that he knew my name, but it transpired that his mother lived in New Leake and had told him all about me. He recognised me because of my black patch.

He produced a litre of sticky orange which I had to drink to line my stomach and give a better scan. I was glad I couldn't taste the stuff.

Soon it was my turn. I have had scans in the past, but this one looked so simple.

I had to be in a certain position, and the radiographer began to line up my hips in the required manner, but he had to start all over again when he realised I was still wearing my skirt.

I had quite recently had a brain scan in Lincoln where I was strapped down, face first, with my arms by my side.

This time I had to place my hands above my head, but first there was supposed to be an injection. I told the doctor that I had had so many injections in the back of my hands that the veins had closed up, so I had to get off the table again to remove my tights so that he could try the injection in my feet.

He made two painful very painful - attempts and I complained, so he said he would try to do it without the injection.

So, with my hands above my head, the bed was pushed into the hole in the middle of the white machine which looked like a giant polo mint. Seventeen pictures were taken one quickly after the other, and then three more.

My arms ached and I was pleased when it was all over and I was taken back to the City Hospital.

Back in my ward, alone, I planned an early night in preparation for the operation next morning. At the head of my bed was the notice 'Nil by mouth'.

I telephoned Pat to tell him that I was first on the next day's 'ops' list, and to tell him, for the millionth time, that I loved him.

The nurses had kept my supper warm, and I was about to eat it when the houseman came in. Looking at the food, probably, I thought, my last decent meal for a while, he said: "You can have your breakfast in the morning."

I looked at him in disbelief.

He continued: "We can't operate. You have secondaries (cancer) in both lungs. I thought you'd like to know that you can still order your breakfast."

I wanted to scream at him: "I don't care about my bloody breakfast."

It was like offering a condemned man food before taking him to the gallows.

I cried a lot that night, but I didn't ring Pat again. It was better that he should have a good night's sleep.

Next morning I refused breakfast!

Soon Mr. Salama came along on a ward visit. He was sorry,

171

he said, but there was nothing he could do. I could go home just as soon as I pleased.

Pat was upset at the news, but saved his tears until we were re-united at Pilgrim Hospital where we went to see Mr. Knowles who seemed taken aback by the report.

The only thing in favour of this damned tumour is that it is a rare, slow-growing type. It does not react to chemotherapy or radiotherapy. Apart from the awful tiredness I had no other symptoms at this time.

Dreadful though the news was, I was boosted by one thing: the impending award of the Freedom of the Borough of Boston.

Before that memorable night, however, there were two more blows. My letter to Uncle Jack was returned: 'Unknown at this address'. Lynda Chalker, at the Foreign Office, had taken the trouble to send the names of cancer specialists in various parts of the world but Mr. Knowles advised against such a trip. I had had the best treatment in the world already.

There was, however, still the Freedom ceremony to look forward to. The cancer that had taken me to the threshold of the biggest honour a town can give, was not going to prevent me from enjoying every minute of the big night, and the build-up to it. With the support of my family, and the kindness of councillors, officers, and friends, it turned out to be every bit as memorable as I hoped it would be.

I loved the tradition and protocol and, although there were so many more people I would have loved to have invited, I was glad the special council meeting was held in Boston's historic council chamber, despite its limited size.

I was the first woman to be made a Freeman of the Borough of Boston, and I cannot tell you what a thrill that was.

I was nervous and excited. It was a super evening. I managed to keep my calm as Councillor John Wright proposed that the Freedom be conferred on me. He said all kinds of flattering things about me and it soon became obvious that he had read part of my autobiography because he mentioned things he would not otherwise have known. Then I remembered that he and George Wheatman, who had helped me with the book, were friends.

172

Councillor Dr. John Wallis said nice things about DOCATEF. I was touched by the warmth and sincerity of both men, and delighted when other councillors added their congratulations.

I had thought a lot about what I would say in reply, but I didn't take along any notes; I always fluffed things when I referred to notes. It was a good chance to say thank you to all my friends, and to let my family know how much they mean to me.

I especially wanted to end by saying: "Pat, I love you". But I couldn't. The tears wouldn't let me. Emotion took over and I sat down.

I thought of my mother, and Pat's mum and dad. They would have been so proud. I was proud too.

As usual I read everything in the newspapers written about the event, and the Target even went to the trouble of publishing a colour photograph of myself and the Mayor.

I think it was through reading the Target that I finally realised the lofty company I was keeping as a Freeman.

They commissioned local historian George Bagley to look back over the years and recall some of the previous recipients of the honour.

He wrote:

> The Honorary Freedom is the highest honour the borough of Boston can bestow. The borough council's decision so to give recognition to cancer victim Lyn Ellis, that courageous fund-raiser, makes history in a number of ways.
>
> Boston has been a good deal more sparing than most ancient boroughs in bestowing its supreme accolade.
>
> Lyn will be the first woman ever to receive it, and the first individual to do so since local government reorganisation in 1974, which resulted in the enlargement of the borough to incorporate the villages of the former Boston Rural District Council area.
>
> Among the earliest recipients were Sir Joseph Banks of Revesby and his colleague Dr. Daniel Carl Solander, the great Swedish botanist. They were voted the Freedom on returning in 1771 from the three-year voyage of discovery undertaken by HMS Endeavour

- the first circumnavigation of the world under the command of James Cook (not yet rated as captain), during which Banks and his companions reached the unknown eastern shores of Australia.

The borough council of the day sought to mark their generous and distinguished pursuits towards the increase of natural knowledge and for the discovery of new countries, so beneficial to the commercial interests of these kingdoms.

Later, of course, for the last eleven years of his life, Banks was Boston's Recorder, an appointment marked by the presentation to him of the portrait of himself which still hangs in Boston Guildhall.

Admiral Lord Horatio Nelson and the now forgotten Sir Richard Calder were granted the Honorary Freedom in 1805, 'for their great and meritorious exertions'. That August, in acknowledging that he had received the Corporation's thanks 'for my conduct during my late command, by which they are pleased to think great advantages to the country have been derived'. Nelson gave this assurance: 'I shall endeavour by my future conduct to preserve the good opinion which they are pleased to entertain of me.'

Two months later, in command of HMS Victory, he made the supreme sacrifice at the battle of Trafalgar. His body was brought home to England for burial, and on the day of his funeral Bostonians filled the 'Stump' for a memorial service to 'the late, ever to be lamented Lord Nelson, a free burgess of this borough'.

In the first (and last) mass ceremony of its kind, the end of the Boer War found the seven surviving members of the 'The Gallant Eight', members of the Rifle Volunteers who had served alongside the Regulars, granted the Honorary Freedom.

They included two brothers, Lance Cpl. John Baxter Kirby and Pte. Ralph Kirby, the others being Lance Sgt. Frank David Emery, Lance Cpl. Oliver Cooper, and Private Charles W Crawley, Meaburn Staniland and Cyril J Mawson.

The resolution that they be so honoured, 'in recognition of their services as Volunteers with the 2nd Battalion of the Lincolnshire Regiment in the South African War', was passed at a special meeting of the Council on the 18th May 1901 – the day on which the last six arrived back in Boston to a heroes' welcome (Ralph Kirby was already home).

Meaburn Staniland was a son of Boston's Town Clerk, Robert William Staniland, and succeeded his father in that post. The father took over again during World War I, in which Meaburn and his brother Geoffrey, both officers, were killed on the Western Front in 1915.

Their father carried on as town clerk into the early 1920s, and duly received the Honorary Freedom on his retirement. Robert William and Meaburn Staniland are the only father and son to have received its highest honour in the history of the borough.

In the last sixty years only eight individuals have been made Honorary Freemen, but the Freedom has been conferred upon RAF Coningsby (in 1962) and the Royal Anglian Regiment (in 1981).

Of the individual recipients, the sole survivor is former long-serving town clerk, Mr Cyril Louis Hoffrock Griffiths, still a regular visitor to the town though he has spent his retirement at Exmouth (Devon).

All the others were members of the borough council, with many years' service to their credit. Of these only Alfred Chester and Arthur Lealand, aldermen both, had not served the mayoral office.

The six ex-Mayors presented with the Freedom scroll were: Tom Kitwood (Mayor in 1906 and '07), Charles Henry Wing (1923), Edward Arthur Bailey (1928), Reuben Salter (1929) – he was Boston's first Labour chief citizen – John Henry Mountain (1944) and James Parkin Roe (1951).

There was a lovely atmosphere that evening. I felt that people were truly pleased for me, but the fact that I had been given the Freedom of the Borough never really hit me until I received a letter which commenced 'Dear Freeman'.

It was an invitation to Boston's Civic Dinner.

175

That was another of the good occasions made possible, ironically, by cancer. Without it I would have been Lyn Who? Because of it I was Lyn Ellis, Freeman of the Borough of Boston. The honour acted as a sedative, but not for long. My health was rather like the weather of 1986. It started badly, had a bright spell, but then slumped back into the doldrums. There were more bad days than good. The pain returned with a vengeance. It was around the area of my nose which became too painful to bear my glasses.

I wore my pirate's patch only in public, then not at all because of the pain.

In June I went back to Pilgrim Hospital and more cancer was removed from under the bridge of my nose. When I left hospital this time it was, for the first time ever, in a wheelchair.

It took me a long time to get back into my stride. I hesitate to say recover, because that word doesn't seem to be in my dictionary. Already cancer is back in my forehead tracing its painful finger further and further along. That in my lungs - touch wood - appears to be growing little, or not at all.

I get tired, oh so tired, very quickly. I feel the cold so keenly and, with the cold, comes that unbearable pain.

Between, say, September and May, all the money we have is spent on fuel in an attempt to keep the house warm enough for me to be comfortable. While others sweat, I shiver, and I hang onto my thermal underwear until well into the middle of summer.

I have to live with the pain, and I try to ignore it as much as possible. It becomes easier with the warmth. Oh, if only we had better weather in England.

Thank goodness for DOCATEF. Without it I would have more time to sit and brood. I think that raising money to help other cancer sufferers has prevented cancer from killing me.

In my heart of hearts I know it will win - but not without a fight.

My life now jumps over the painful spells to the stepping stones of satisfying achievements.

There was the £200,000 target for DOCATEF, now achieved: the fund's seventh birthday in October: an invitation to the Woman of the Year luncheon in London: and publication of this, my autobiography, which I hope, in its humble way, will encourage others to fight, and maybe master, cancer.

We are into 1987 now; there have been more stays in Pilgrim hospital, more surgery, more - much more - pain. But the fight has continued.

I have learned to live one day at a time and, because of my fund, and because of the undiminishing love of Pat and my family, I know I didn't have cancer for nothing.

o